How To Plan & Conduct A Successful Meeting

Myron Gordon, Ph.D.

Introduction by
Henry Kressel, Vice-President, RCA

 Sterling Publishing Co., Inc.   New York

Library of Congress Cataloging in Publication Data

Gordon, Myron J.
　　How to plan and conduct a successful meeting.

　　Originally published as: Making meetings more productive. c1981.
　　Includes index.
　　1. Communication in management.　2. Meetings.
I. Title.
[HF5718.G67　1985]　　　658.4'563　　　85-9851
ISBN 0-8069-6256-9 (pbk.)

Published in 1985 by Sterling Publishing Co., Inc.
Two Park Avenue, New York, N.Y. 10016
Originally published in hardcover under
the title "Making Meetings More Productive" © 1981
by Sterling Publishing Co., Inc.
Distributed in Australia by Capricorn Book Co. Pty. Ltd.
Unit 5C1 Lincoln St., Lane Cove, N.S.W. 2066
Distributed in the United Kingdom by Blandford Press
Link House, West Street, Poole, Dorset BH15 ILL, England
Distributed in Canada by Oak Tree Press Ltd.
% Canadian Manda Group, P.O. Box 920, Station U
Toronto, Ontario, Canada M8Z 5P9
Manufactured in the United States of America
All rights reserved

Contents

Foreword 9

Introduction 10

1:
The Basic Ingredient of a Meeting—You! 12
    Experiencing   14
    Sharing   14
    Putting Together   15
    Applying   16
    Evaluating   17
    Experimenting   17
    Memo   18

2:
Removing Blind Spots 19
    Key Definitions   19
    Obstacles to Achievement   21
    Realities, Not Myths   23
    Memo   24

3:
Straight Thinking about Meetings 25
    Belief in Working Together   26
    Choice of Leader   28
    Number and Mix   28
    Agreeing and Deciding   29
    A Rigorous Meeting   30
    What Centering Can Do   31
    Memo   33

4:
What Kind of Leader Are You? 34
    The Three Types of Leaders   34
    Styles of Leadership   40
    Moving Toward   41
    Moving Against   42
    Moving Away From   43
    Basic Moves   45
    Leading with Skill and Style   47
    Memo   48

5:
In the Beginning 49
    Problem Facing   49
    Advance Planning   50
    Plan of Meeting   51
    The Host   52
    A Contract with Large Letters   53
    Ground Rules for a Centered Meeting   55
    Memo   58

6:
The Leader Takes Hold 59
    From Task to Theme   59
    The Job Is Launched   61
    Telling How It's Done   62
    The Leader Is Neutral   63
    Dealing with Distractions   64
    How the Ground Rules Promote the Meeting   65
    Memo   67

7:
Four Elements of a Meeting 68
    The Member Component   68
    The Team Component   69
    The Work-Goal Factor   69
    The Organization Factor   69
    Working with the System   70
    Memo   71

8:
Setting the Focus 72
    Foreground and Background   72
    Task in Foreground   73
    Task in Background   76
    Memo   78

9:
Every Element Gets a Chance 79
    Identifying Neglect and Exaggeration   79
    How Balancing Works   81
    The Balancing Act of a Centered Meeting   83
    Memo   84

10:
Your Inner Zone 85
    Filtering   85
    Self-Expression from the Core   87
    Memo   88

11:
Your Best Foot Forward 89
    You've Got to Be Believed   91
    Opposite Ends Work Together   91
    One Part of Me/The Other Part of Me   92
    The Body Speaks Loudly   93
    Memo   97

12:
Removing Communication Roadblocks 98
    Preventing Blocked Ideas and Messages   99
    Seven Common Communication Blocks   99–103
    Removing Communication Roadblocks   104
    Memo   105

13:
More Than You Think 106
    Rational Thinking   106
    Irrational Beliefs about Meetings   107
    Sensing and Feeling   108
    "I"-Behavior   110
    "We"-Behavior   111
    "It"-Behavior   111
    Memo   112

14:
We Are All the Same—but Different 113
    A Day at the Circus   114
    Skills for Awareness, Decision and Action   118
    Memo   119

15:
"I Said, You Said . . ." 120
    Technique of Cultivating   120
    Technique of Experimenting   120
    Technique of Weeding   120
    Task/Theme: Morale-Building   122
    Memo   128

16:
How to Shape a Meeting 129
   Information Meeting   130
   Problem-Solving Meeting   130
   Creative Meeting   132
   Teaching and Training Meeting   134
   Memo   138

17:
Stimulating Productivity 139
   Exercises in Productivity   140
   The Play in Meetings   142
   Managing Conflict   143
   Memo   144

18:
Your Associates and How to Work with Them 145
   Maturity Levels   146
   Working Types   148
   Memo   151

19:
The Midpoint Checkup 152
   The Leader   152
   Team-Building and Maintenance   154
   What to Do at the Midpoint Checkup   155
   Memo   157

20:
First Aid for Meetings in Trouble 158
   The Weak "I"   159
   The Limping Team   161
   The Fading Task   164
   Memo   165

21:
How to End a Meeting Successfully 166
   The Work Done   166
   The People Who Did It   167
   Record of Meeting   168
   Memo   169

Glossary 170

Index 177

Foreword

This book is written to help you improve the management, conduct and productivity of meetings. If you are a company president (or hope to be one!), a foundation executive, vice-president of personnel, a manager at any level of business, a teacher or supervisor in our schools and colleges—anyone who makes things happen in business, government, institutions, and community—then this book was written for you.

Most of the chapters are designed for both leaders and members—the one can look over the shoulder of the other. The leader who understands how to participate is wiser and more sensitive. The member who works at maintaining a meeting becomes a stronger member—and makes the leader more effective as well.

The case histories and examples given are composites of meetings I have led, attended or heard about in the past 20 years.

I wish to express my gratitude to Dr. Ruth C. Cohn, my teacher and friend, whose concepts and applications of her Theme-Centered Interaction have influenced a generation of group leaders all over the world. The "centered" meeting in this book is derived from her method.

Norman J. Liberman and I have such a close working relationship that a number of the ideas in this book have, no doubt, been written in my handwriting but with his voice. For his brotherly generosity, bountiful intellect and great sensitivity, I shall always be grateful.

Introduction

Effective face-to-face communications at meetings are essential to build and maintain successful organizations. The larger the organization the more difficult the task of making the best possible use of time spent at meetings.

It is primarily at meetings, involving at some time several levels of the organization, that the unity of purpose is forged which is needed to meet objectives. The give-and-take between leader and subordinates makes the participants feel an integral part of the organization and thus promotes initiative and creative problem-solving. Organizations which lack the participation developed at meetings also lack the morale necessary to develop a winning spirit.

The resolution of conflicts at meetings is particularly crucial in promoting cooperation between segments of the organization with differing objectives. For example, areas of potential conflict easily arise between units representing separate profit centers. It is obvious that the needs of each unit manager to maximize his or her profits must be reconciled with the overall profit objectives of the organization, but building a team where everybody feels a winner when the organization succeeds is the greatest challenge facing management. The careful structuring and timing of meetings are essential to this goal. The leader must understand individual motives and personalities and control those all-too-human traits which sometimes lead to needless strife.

Effective leaders learn to use meetings to build successful teams. Strategies and objectives are defined and explained, progress is monitored and timely decisions are made to shift resources as conditions change. Well-run meetings lead to increased productivity by promoting cooperation. When poorly run, they not only are a waste of time in themselves, but lead to further meetings—which ultimately tie up the most productive members of the organization in frustrating efforts to chart a path. Useful meetings require advance planning, a careful selection of the members and monitoring during the meeting to prevent a loss of definition of what the meeting is trying to accomplish.

Effective meetings are, unfortunately, too rare. As a result, key experts in organizations find their time wasted at the expense of productive problem solving. There are several major reasons for the poor use of meeting time.

First, the leader all too frequently is interested in the short-term meeting objective—reaching a decision or formulating a plan—and neglects the process for achieving the longer-term objective of team building. Thus, when the meeting is over, the participants feel mistreated. Second, people are distracted by individual problems and therefore find it difficult to participate in the group activity. Third, differences in status among the participants inhibit the freedom of exchange.

In view of the impediments to useful communications, it is not surprising that people protect what they perceive to be their own interests. Unfortunately, this behavior may be detrimental to the interests of the organization and thus, ultimately, to the interests of the participants. The procedures and concepts discussed apply to all organizations. The book addresses the needs of the leader and members and ways of promoting teamwork.

The author successfully launches his many practical and cogent suggestions from a wide and firm theoretical base. In this way he is able to deliver to the reader both the tools and the means of using them in productive ways.

Henry Kressel,
Vice-President, RCA

1:
The Basic Ingredient of a Meeting—You!

Make your meetings more productive by starting with the basic ingredient: Yourself! You attend meetings frequently, and you've seen things go wrong at every session. Perhaps you wanted to step in and help by: redirecting the flow of energy; expressing a cogent argument or practical solution, or even by just telling a joke . . . but you didn't. You became bored or paralyzed with fear or lost and confused. Or did you, in fact, speak up, but too loudly and too soon?

The very nature of a meeting is artificial and complicated. As a member, you need to be as prepared—not *armed*, but prepared—as an athlete entering a tournament or a student taking a final exam. And by preparation it is not meant knowing only facts and details—but knowing yourself, and knowing people, too. Consider these answers, given by employees, to a personnel director's question: "If we held a training session for meeting members, what would you like—or need—to learn?"

1. How to be true to myself as well as an appropriate meeting member.
2. How to get help and encouragement without leaning too hard on others with my problems.
3. How to connect with a leader whose style is entirely different from my own.
4. How to be a member of the team as a whole while avoiding the formation of cliques.

5. How to use logical thinking without choking off creative imagination.
6. How to get across my own opinions while also giving way to others.
7. How to define the basic operations of a member and how to carry them out.

J. W. Pfeiffer and J. E. Jones suggested in their *Annual Handbook for Group Facilitators* that being an effective meeting member requires five basic actions, to which we've added a sixth, that not only can you perform but with which you're already familiar. They are:

- Experiencing
- Sharing
- Putting together
- Applying
- Evaluating
- Experimenting

Here is an illustration of three different personality types and how these basic actions are used by them.

Underconfident. Hector, a competent but passive computer programmer, always looks drained after a meeting—even when harmony and progress were achieved.

"Sitting through a meeting *is* stressful," Hector insists, "because of your exposure and the unpredictability of everyone else." He rarely feels confident about what he says or does at meetings, although he is fully at ease at home with his wife and children.

Confident. Ethan, a reporter in a large news organization, is an assertive but yielding person at home and on the job. Rarely hostile or defensive about criticism, he has high self-esteem and a genuine sense of pleasure with others. Usually, he is quite certain of what he wants to say and do at meetings.

Overconfident. Jenny, a field worker for a governmental aid program, has boundless charm and energy. But she makes too many wry comments and oversteps her bounds with both peers and those in charge. She wants to do things her own way and makes it clear that she doesn't like to be corrected. (Once, when her boss insisted that this time she was wrong, she ran from the meeting in tears.) At meetings, she gives the impression of being very sure of herself—always.

As you read the following basic operations and case illustrations, try to give yourself a preliminary rating. You might ask: "What qualities do I have in common with these people? Which should I try to drop or build up?"

Experiencing

You experience things and collect data about what's going on through thoughts, feelings and senses. How much and how well you take it all in depends on how good a receiver you are. When you receive accurately, you can react fully and appropriately to what is actually going on.

Hector ("I'm Not Sure") fears the consequences of a meeting. His reasoning is: "Why give suggestions? The supervisor will just consider them as an attack." As a result, Hector finds it safer to see and hear less—maintaining uncertainty about things going on around him—as a way of avoiding assertiveness. Instead of considered opinions, forceful suggestions, Hector often asks, "What did you say?" If Hector possessed more self-esteem and gave himself more credit, his self-confidence would be greater. Then he'd be more open to taking in and dealing with situations around him. However, Hector's mousey behavior is somewhat offset by sharp thinking about problems of the department and an unusual sensitivity for the feelings of others.

Sharing

You share the data of a meeting with others who are doing the same thing. This makes you a participant-observer. You can shift gears from observing to participating/sharing. This kind of exchange calls for sending and receiving skills—knowing just how your words and your information are getting across, as well as receiving just what the other person means. Sharing also requires your willingness to aim for relating and cooperating, rather than winning.

ETHAN ("I'm Quite Certain") is talking to a news editor at the weekly staff meeting.

EDITOR: Well, it looks like we'll have to take on an additional reporter or else we'll keep missing out to International News.

ETHAN: I recall that Bob and Jean were saying there's a problem

with our telex machines and that's what is holding up our releases.
EDITOR: Are you saying that hiring another reporter won't help?
ETHAN: No, not really. It's just that I thought Bob and Jean had a good point about the old telex breaking down all the time ... but they didn't seem to want to blame maintenance.
EDITOR: Thanks for bringing out this angle.

Ethan's basic security is a valuable asset. He functions effectively both in and out of meetings. Ethan's popularity and ability to blend his ideas with others go hand in hand. At the above meeting, Ethan got to the crux of the problem without showing up the editor who is known as a rather touchy boss. Ethan was aware of some pertinent information and brought it out skillfully. As a sidelight, it's interesting that sometimes he feels uneasy about the "strokes" of admiration he gets from all sides. He fears that sustaining this public role of the "great guy" will become a burden. "Will I make a fool of myself next time? I sure like the strokes, but will I be able to survive the ridicule if I fall flat on my face?"

Putting Together

You put together the pieces of all the data which serve the purposes of the meeting. Attention and concentration help you retain all those small but necessary details. Once you digest them, you can use them for the task/theme of the meeting. Careful advance preparation—familiarizing yourself with the facts and issues—is a must.

JENNY ("I'm Very Sure"), the field worker, attended a meeting of another governmental department, also dealing with aid. While she knew the policies of her own department, she knew very little about the policies operating at this meeting. Yet she was super confident and her overconfidence made it difficult for her to put data together carefully.

JESSE: We'll need a lot more information before I can agree to a change in the way a small business can apply for a loan.

JENNY: I realize there's a lot to correlate, but as I've just outlined, my department has already adopted an improved policy about processing the applications. I think you should adopt our procedure; it's far superior to your own.

ANOTHER MEMBER: I would be in favor of the policy we

came up with at this meeting, even though Jenny has brought us the benefit of her department's ideas.

JENNY: OK. But you're only going to come to the same conclusion in the end that we did, anyway.

Jenny tends to be impatient and hasty about drawing conclusions. This makes her gloss over important details. Were she better at putting pieces together, Jenny wouldn't have made the last awkward remark, which went against the grain of the others. It marked her as an arrogant "snip."

Applying

You apply generalizations to situations outside the meeting by bridging present and future. To do this requires hope, daring, excitement and energy. Your apprehensions must be overcome. If you see a meeting as relatively "safe" but get anxious at the thought of going on to post-meeting action and implementation, your decisions may reflect excessive caution. It's difficult to be daring and energetic when you're fearful. That's why it's so important to confront these fears and subdue them with feelings of self-esteem.

No one can deny that Hector ("I'm Not Sure") is full of original ideas. But as soon as he has to apply his ideas to definite solutions, he finds excuses to back down.

HECTOR: There are countless medium-sized companies still doing their accounting with computers from the '50s. We have just the right kind of setup to take care of something like this.

SALES REPRESENTATIVE: Hector, could you meet with some of the salespeople next week and help them with a sales presentation manual directed to chief accountants in the pharmaceutical field?

HECTOR: (Looking the other way) Thanks, but I don't know anything about selling. I'd be glad to program the job once you get the contract, but I can't imagine how I could be of help with the manual.

Hector was given the chance to move up to an interesting interdepartmental project. Unfortunately, his limitation in being able to picture himself in new situations stopped him from following through and applying his own good suggestion. By not using creative vision Hector could not bridge present and future.

Evaluating

You evaluate with open-minded questions about how well the work is proceeding, what is happening to you and whether things could be done better. This activity requires your willingness to take an undefensive position when you become aware of flaws in what you have done. It also takes ability to provide supportive feedback to others about their work.

ETHAN ("I'm Quite Certain") usually takes an active part at meetings. Others trust him, not only for his accepting manner, but also for his consistency. He has a way of bringing together his private self—the way he experiences himself—with the way he comes across to others. Here is an exchange at a recent meeting:

EDITOR: Let's have a change of pace, lean back and see how we've been doing so far.

ETHAN: There were a few times when I felt it was hard to jump into the conversation. It felt too much like competition. Trouble is, it made me lose track of what the speaker was saying.

EDITOR: Did this happen to anyone else?

MEL: Sure, it happened to me, too, now that Ethan mentioned it. I'd like to figure out why I felt it was necessary to keep pushing so hard to break in. I think that in a competitive atmosphere, I feel I have to fight hard to get a little recognition.

Ethan has a healthy, questioning, open-minded attitude. Being "quite certain" of his perceptions and conclusions, he's free to give accurate and useful reactions. In this case, he was secure enough to word an evaluation in self-critical terms—which easily gave an impetus to others to join in.

Experimenting

You experiment and take risks with new forms of behavior to stretch your limits. Without recognizing changing situations—and new ways of dealing with them—an organization cannot hope for survival. This mode of behavior at meetings leads to creative combinations of ideas for efficiency, productivity and avoidance of the dread disease "hardening of the categories!"

JENNY ("I'm Very Sure") often produces "sparks" at meetings. Her know-it-all manner grates on some people's nerves. Others say she has such a quick mind that she gets impatient with anyone who can't keep up with her. On balance, though Jenny's insecurities make her hunger after approval, she is also an imaginative and fluid thinker whose assets could be harnessed at any meeting.

Jenny is a good example of someone whose thinking, after taking flight, comes down to earth with novel combinations of ideas. Her overconfidence even might be considered as an asset when experimental and creative ideas are called for.

MEMO

SUBJECT: What the member wants to know about the basics of a meeting.

1. Knowing <u>what</u> to do is sometimes easier than knowing <u>how</u> because of the artificial—and even confusing—nature of a meeting.

2. There are a number of basic actions you can perform to be a productive member at all meetings. They are: Experiencing, Sharing, Putting Together, Applying, Evaluating and Experimenting.

3. These actions should be tailored to your personality type. Of the many possible types, three have been devised for purposes of illustration.

2:
Removing Blind Spots

When you call a meeting—or attend one—you expect to pool your abilities and solve common problems, dilemmas and issues. That's the ideal; the reality is somewhat (and sometimes quite a bit) different. Gathering together a group of people at a specific time and place will not, by itself, guarantee a productive, successful meeting.

There are specific reasons why some meetings succeed and others fail. But first, key definitions need to be understood, built-in obstacles to the success of a meeting removed and myths about the nature of a meeting exploded.

Key Definitions

A **meeting** is a structured and planned situation where people work together in a give-and-take relationship to do one or more of the following:

- Present
- Explore and share information
- Solve problems
- Expedite decisions
- Create new ideas and procedures
- Teach
- Train
- Evaluate

The groups holding these meetings go by such names as:
- Team
- Committee
- Unit
- Department
- Task force
- Interest group

The value of a meeting should not be limited to the situation alone. The experience should also serve as a springboard for everyone to improve his or her work and relationships in the organization between meetings.

The **leader** is the person designated to run the meeting. Most often, leaders of meetings are those who, by virtue of their position in the organization, are most expert or knowledgeable about the matter on the agenda. But frequently, leaders are selected "from the ranks" because of personal or technical skills in leading group discussions.

A **member** is someone who belongs at the meeting, hopefully because he or she *wants* to be there and because the member has something to offer to the work of the specific meeting.

There are two kinds of **teams.** One team meets regularly to review and evaluate the work of their unit, to touch base with each other and to perform various kinds of housekeeping and maintenance. The second kind refers to gatherings—not limited in composition by organizational structure—to accomplish specific tasks. The session or sessions last until the job is done. Teams work best when they run like one organ; not cracked, split or broken into separate parts.

The **elements of a meeting** are:

Person-Solving. Giving—or receiving—help, avoiding personal problem orientation, getting across ideas, merging with the team while maintaining self-identity, maintaining flexibility in choices of behavior, working comfortably with authority.

Team-Solving. Developing the team's skills of observation to enhance, shed light on, correct, or improve the maintenance of the teamwork.

Work-Solving. Defining, solving and following up on the problem or issue through selected techniques.

Organization-Solving. Encouraging (or sabotaging) the effectiveness of the meeting through organizational influence and setting. Morale, support, purpose, clarity and sincerity are all linked to the background or structure of a meeting.

What Comes Naturally

You come to a meeting already armed with skills which you've used successfully in other situations. The secret is finding, improving, developing and applying these skills for meetings.

These functions include a number of actions described by J. W. Pfeiffer and J. E. Jones in the *Annual Handbook for Group Facilitators* (1972-1978).

- You *experience* things and collect data about what's going on through thoughts, feelings, senses, actions and will.
- You *share* this data with others doing the same things at the same time.
- You *put together* the pieces of all this data to serve the purposes of the meeting.
- You *apply* these generalizations to situations outside the meeting —by bridging present and future.
- You *evaluate* with open-minded questions what is happening to you, whether things could be done better, how you could react differently and how well the work is proceeding.
- You *experiment* and take risks with new forms of behavior to stretch your limits.

Obstacles

One reason the potentials of a meeting are not often achieved is that we know more about the theory of good meetings than about carrying it into practice. Then, too, it's tempting for an organization to use meetings for productivity alone, neglecting the opportunities for staff development and two-way communication.

This general downgrading or misuse of meetings has a bad effect on the way people participate. No wonder we hear the common complaints, "Still more talking?" or, "Is this discussion necessary?"

Besides the obstacles hampering management from maximizing the potential of meetings, there are difficulties inherent in the very nature of people trying to work together. Wilfred Bion, a pioneer in the theory of group behavior, observed in his book, *Experience In Groups*, three typical ways in which members are held back:

1. The leader is seen as an all-knowing figure, providing unlimited support.

The solution is to recognize and counter your tendencies to act helpless. Don't allow someone else to take over when independent behavior is called for.

2. The group takes certain exaggerated and unnecessary actions to preserve itself, as though its existence is more important than the team's job. These actions take the form of fighting a member who has "let down" the group, or of joining others in a "flight" from the work of the meeting.

As a solution, increase your awareness of these wasteful, group-preserving movements. Remind yourself of the main theme and purpose of the meeting—the reason why you are there.

3. Members pair up with others, seemingly to further the work, but in fact, get away from the main productive thrust of the team.

Look carefully at this pairing. You'll see that it's unrealistic to expect big results from the work of this member/pair, while pushing the work of the team as a whole into the background. "Twosomes" should be viewed as potentially injurious diversions from the major work of the meeting.

These three tendencies, found by Bion, easily can drag down a meeting unless they are checked. The actions by leaders and members outlined in the ground rules (Chapter 5) will resist these regressive pulls.

Another counter-productive force at meetings is when the members—all adults, of course—are treated like a group of children. The agenda is served up by leader and organizer (parent), often without consultation of the members (children). Members sit in rows shaped like a classroom or around a table which tapers toward the leader. The final decisions are made without adequate recognition of the member's contribution. Although, presumably, their ideas are needed, grown men and women are squelched in these "parent-child" interactions.

Thrown into this child's world, members often find themselves either competing for the leader's attention or ganging up on the leader in surreptitious ways. The antidote? Strive to develop adult-to-adult relationships while still maintaining authority. In turn, members can try to synthesize the following:

- Behave in a self-revealing yet impersonal manner.
- Be absolutely sincere and act appropriately in the context of the meeting.
- Adopt a combined attitude of easygoing, relaxed playfulness and attentive concentration.

Realities, Not Myths

There are other obstacles to meetings—myths which need to be exploded.

MYTH: The organization believes that merely by putting together leader, members and agenda, a successful meeting will be created.

REALITY: Don't assume that the meeting is like a beehive working automatically in the way nature intended. You work with *learned* patterns of behavior and with structures you've devised which are difficult to control. This is why you need to learn how to adapt and function better while under the stress and strain of a meeting.

MYTH: The organization maintains that a meeting doesn't differ from other forms of work involving groups of people. Therefore, no special preparation is required.

REALITY: The meeting is an activity different from other forms of work. You're plunged into an experience of magnified exposure, proximity, competition and other pressures. Orientation and preparation are essential.

MYTH: Productivity depends largely on the leader who, like a computer, receives, sorts out, classifies and redirects ideas as they emerge from participants.

REALITY: Productivity depends not so much on the "all-knowing leader," but on the power of individuals to work on the task without opting for the easier road of avoidance.

MYTH: Feelings are neither to be seen nor heard.

REALITY: A meeting runs on feeling as well as on thinking. While some feelings are better left underground, others are needed out in the open to "lubricate" the exchange of ideas. (This should not include the use of feelings for self-gratification at the expense of others.) Another abuse of feelings is the "shut-off," which occurs when you're about to give genuine, frank feedback to another team member. Be aware that some people are so afraid of the possibilities of expression that they shut off or squelch the speaker.

MYTH: The events and conclusions about a meeting are usually agreed upon by those who attend.

REALITY: You leave a meeting with impressions differing from every other member. In his studies, Dr. C. Argyris pointed to a gap in what you experience and recall. At the end of meetings, there isn't that "mythical consensus."

MYTH: What you see and hear at a meeting is *all* that goes on.

REALITY: The air is full of unheard and unseen messages. Between-the-lines communications can be useful, if you can bring them out into the open. Otherwise, they create static.

```
                  MEMO
     SUBJECT: Getting past the blind spots to a
     clear view of the meeting.
        1. Meetings offer the promise of achieve-
     ment but,like other mechanisms,they break down.
        2. As a prerequisite to understanding why
     some meetings succeed and others fail, you
     must be clear in using the key terms:
     Meetings, leader, members, teams, work-
     solving, person-solving, team-solving and
     organization-solving.
        3. Another key to successful meetings is
     to understand—and remove—the psychological
     obstacles which prevent mature functioning.
        4. Other impediments, in the form of faulty
     attitudes and myths about meetings, can be
     dispelled when looked at realistically.
```

3:
Straight Thinking about Meetings

Here are some of the main ideas about meetings that can make the difference between productive and wasteful sessions.

Connecting the Minds

A meeting really is a *meeting of the minds* around a common task. Effective communication means lifting the veil between yourself and others. In Eric Berne's *The Structure and Dynamics of Organizations and Groups*, the transactional analysis motto says: "I'm OK, you're all right, and the situation seems welcome." This is a good place to start. Repeat it over and over to yourself until it's part of you. Once this is done, you'll find that your thoughts and feelings flow more easily—and that other people, in turn, respond with more understanding and support.

The circle of communication is now complete. Each instance of understanding and support enables you to feel better about yourself, others and the situation.

After the veil between you and others is lifted and communication flows smoothly, you can go forward and maintain a supportive climate—or slip backward with a defensive one. Jack Gibb in *T-Group Theory and Laboratory Methods* gave some valuable insights to watch for:

♦ If you are seen as a judge, always *evaluating* others, they'll shy away from open expression.

- If you try to *control* the meeting, rather than engage in the *work* of the meeting, you'll be met with resistance.
- If you're seen as *spontaneous*, rather than *devious*, you'll receive open responses in return.
- If you try to *put yourself in the other person's position*, rather than remaining neutral to his or her expression of feeling, you strengthen the rapport.
- If you maintain an *equal attitude*, rather than one of *superiority*, others are more apt to be open and responsible.
- If you keep your *mind open to all sides of an issue*, leaving room for differences, you'll encounter less resistance.

Belief in Working Together

A meeting is kept alive by the beliefs of its members and leader. What are some of these beliefs?

* The meeting is a force for democracy and fairness. Its purpose is maximum productivity by the team, with equal recognition for equal participation. Undemocratic features — invariably present in an organization—must take a back seat. Even if a leader "knows better" about certain matters, the combination of leader *and* members lets everyone "know" even better.
* There's no contradiction in stating your point of view on one hand, and being interdependent on the other. You need your own thoughts *and* the thoughts of your colleagues.
* People feel good about being reached out to and contacted in a work situation. This makes you feel secure enough to want to move ahead and achieve.
* The meeting gives opportunities for personal expansion and growth. For example, where you are *thinking* too much, someone is always there to turn your attention to *experiencing*. Where you're basking in your private world of feelings, someone will serve as a model for *action and enactment*.
* A common task kept in center focus can unify even where differences and conflicts exist. Differences in thought and temperament, when acknowledged and valued, enrich the work of the group.
* It's possible to defer outside allegiances in favor of the current team effort. You can be a good member of two groups at once, even if there are overlapping areas of conflict.

- Competing has its place, but *relating*—not winning—should be the basic meeting activity. Relating not only to other individuals, but also to the other conditions at the meeting. The other channels you should be in tune with are: Welfare of the team and meeting; the state and condition of the task, and policies of the organization.

Mark Lee, a modest yet forceful research engineer in electronics, drives himself almost without letup when at his own desk. With colleagues, he's somewhat competitive (though rarely combative). "But a meeting is a horse of another color entirely," Mark says. "Anyone who runs it as a race—with winners and losers—is going to get a lot of tense, keyed-up people, but no positive results."

Mark goes along with the flow at a meeting, concentrating on whatever seems most relevant. "This is the right way to play it at meetings. I know it is even though I'm not a meeting expert. I just look at the results." He gives and gets "results" because everyone knows he can be counted on to relate to team members. At meetings he steers clear of competition. He offers ideas freely—even when he's outside his immediate range of expertise and can't count on getting a "high-score."

- At a well-run meeting, when your thoughts and your imagination are combined with those of everyone else, the results become greater than the sum of an individual member's thinking. (It's sort of like the axiom that "the whole is larger than the sum of its parts.") You may ask a fair question: "Did the brilliant Einstein, Darwin and Freud get their timeless results at group meetings?" Not very often. Yet, much of their work was influenced by group efforts—the written and spoken scientific dialogues of others before them.

The special advantage of making decisions in groups is shown in J. Hall's famous "Lost on the Moon" assignment. (*American Behavioral Science Training Laboratories*, 1970.) The following problem is given to a group at a meeting:

> A space crew has crash-landed on the moon and must get back to the waiting mother ship. Only a few survival aids were salvaged; 15 in all. They include items such as a box of matches, tanks of oxygen, and so forth.
>
> Everyone at the meeting is asked to rate the importance of the 15 items. Scores are based on NASA's Space Survival Unit deci-

sions. First, everyone is asked to rate the aids on his or her own. Then group decisions are asked for.

When the individual results are compared to the group results, the higher scores are usually those obtained by consensus. Thus, at meetings often you see that the *combined* individual effort is greater than the sum of its parts.

Choice of Leader

There are certain meetings (such as those run by school boards) where the leader/chairperson is recognized as an authority. However, this leader doesn't have the final responsibility of making the decision. Decision-by-vote falls to all those present or to their delegates.

The other type of meeting is run by a leader who has authority over the participants and who may, in turn, have to report to others higher up. In this case, it *is* up to the leader to make the final decision. The power of the one ultimate decision-maker can be softened by varying the leadership occasionally—by inviting a person from the ranks who's skilled in leading. Even if you hold a position of authority, there are times when it's good to leave the "piloting" to a member of the organization with leadership skills. This frees you to contribute more to the substance of a meeting, while someone else takes over the "captain's" responsibilities. However, the ultimate responsibility for making the decision would still remain with you.

This participant role also avoids the objection that a "boss" discourages initiative and induces apathy by conditioning members to appease the authority. (As an added bonus to the organization, the non-authority conducting a meeting is also receiving valuable training for leadership.)

Despite these advantages it's still simplest and most practical for the person in authority to call and chair a meeting.

Number and Mix

You should attend a meeting for specific reasons, such as: To think things over; get things done, and weigh alternate approaches to a shared problem. The meeting may be limited in number of sessions or ongoing; consisting of those in the same unit or from various units—but you all should have a common interest.

A group of five to 15 is big enough to stimulate different points of view and to bring out a range of talent, yet small enough to encourage individual performance. With between 15 and 20 members, the supply of energy and ideas is increased. The danger here is that the more outgoing members take more time than the less assertive but equally productive members. To work with larger groups efficiently, subdivide the group and encourage parallel discussions. Ask the smaller groups to report back to the whole meeting after a short while. The result? A more enthusiastic and larger representation of individual voices.

Agreeing and Deciding

Boiled down to its essentials, a meeting consists of a series of agreements and disagreements about which the group makes decisions. Many agreements flow informally with the mood, pace, timing and composition of members. Others, such as agreement on the ground rules (see Chapter 5) are based on certain formal, agreed-upon conditions spelled out by the leader.

Here are some common methods for agreeing and deciding. (Several were described by E. H. Schein in *Process Consultation: Its Role in Organization Development.*)

The Slide. This is a common but often unnoticed method. Someone mentions an idea, which is followed by another member's suggestion. This process continues until the group gravitates toward one decision which it supports.

The Voting Booth. This is also known as "last resort voting." It is resorted to when differences cannot be resolved. These differences are generally understood and tolerated. However, those who are voted down feel that they have "lost" the round.

The Railroad. When a leader or members have a preconception or bias about an issue, they may insist others see it their way. They'll mount crafty maneuvers to override even a majority opinion. For example, the leader may say, "If no one objects, let's get on to the next point without wasting time discussing this any longer. I'll take care of it myself. Now, Tamar and Eve, what were you saying?"

The Hilltop. The leader sees himself or herself as having the final say and know-how to implement the decision. High on a "hilltop," the leader may take into account the deliberations of the members, but follows his or her own inclinations.

The Perfect Circle. Not easily attainable—and not even necessary—this is the unanimous decision. Everyone present agrees fully on the course of action in terms of its benefits to the organization, its policy and members.

The Rainbow. Known as "consensus," this kind of agreement is described by Schein as a psychological state which says the following:

> I understand what most of you would like to do. I personally would not do it your way, but I feel that you understand—yet disagree—with my alternative suggestion. I've had sufficient opportunity to sway you to my point of view, but clearly haven't been able to do so. Therefore, I'll gladly go along with what most of you wish to do.

The key to consensus is flexibility. No one insists upon maintaining a point of view at all costs. Instead, it's compared carefully with others and, if necessary, modified. Disagreement can be converted into agreement if the factions are willing to find and accept another solution. Different points of view are made into the stuff out of which consensus is fashioned.

Clearly, the first choice is consensus of all present. This method has many advantages, particularly that everyone emerges from the meeting feeling a part of the outcome.

A Rigorous Meeting

The best meeting has rigorous requirements—a meeting where leader and member carry out a number of difficult do's and dont's.

In a joint study by social psychologists and an economist (A. O. Hirschman: *Exit, Voice and Loyalty: Responses in Terms, Organizations and States*), it was found that the more rigorous and demanding the requirements for membership, the more the participant will like the meeting and its members. A second benefit found was that the participant will become more active in improving the group.

In the same study it was learned that where meetings don't occupy a position of importance—where they're not considered to be matters of serious business—they deteriorate in quality. Members assume that there are other competing ways in which people work together, prestige is attained and decisions made. So, even while attending, they have one foot in the exit doorway—they don't participate wholeheartedly. The next pitfall follows: Where there are these other "better channels," members won't raise their voices to complain or correct what may be going wrong at the meeting.

Flexibility

Everyone knows that time is wasted when too many, or the wrong people, attend a meeting. It's less well known that a meeting can be made more efficient when everyone understands equally what type of meeting it is. For instance, important facts have to be reported and digested before a national sales conference; a foreign service unit needs to learn the social customs of the new country; a group of research biologists have to take an entirely new view of their data and plans for further experimentation because of a setback in results. These meetings have separate requirements. Different types of meetings dictate somewhat different attitudes and pace. As a result, you must be flexible. You must learn how to shift gears appropriately.

There are four basic types of meetings:

1. Presenting and sharing information.
2. Problem-solving and decision-making.
3. Creating new ideas and procedures.
4. Teaching and training.

What Centering Can Do

Centering is a way of concentrating and using the forces of a meeting to best advantage. When you're centered, you're acutely aware of inner experiences and outer stimuli. In a related way, *centering* can be used by leader and members to shape a meeting, raising it to a high level of effectiveness and productivity.

These are highlights of how a meeting can be made *centered*:

1. Special ground rules trigger your potential while reducing the obstacles and anxieties that attend every meeting. These ground rules comprise a contract of behavior which, when followed, allows you to respond sincerely, sensitively and appropriately. It also makes it possible for you to trust that others will do the same.

2. The task is expanded to a task-theme, allowing you to join your thoughts and feelings to the theme more creatively. This task-theme is defined and developed as the leader shows members how they can relate to the job in their own special ways.

3. Equal importance is given to *work, member, team* and *organization*. In this way the task, at center, is being shaped by *all* the forces of a meeting.

4. The meeting is a system in which all parts are connected and mutually affected by whatever happens. That's why you're asked to pay attention to your behavior and how this affects the others and the task.

CENTERING AND ITS EFFECTS ON MEMBER AND MEETING

Ways of Centering	What It Does for Productivity
1. Follow special ground rules.	Focuses on task Encourages self-expression and independence Gives structure Emphasizes listening
2. Convert task into a broad task-theme.	Gives you a chance to think about and deal with the task in unique ways. Allows you to connect well with the task.
3. Give all parts of a meeting equal weight.	This is how you can stay in touch with the four forces: work, member, team and organization.
4. Treat meeting as a connected series of events and processes.	Happenings are seen as multi-dimensional. Whatever is said or done has a ripple effect.

MEMO

SUBJECT: What you know in advance about certain positive beliefs and practices is essential. It will add to your commitment, confidence and ultimate success as leader and member.

1. These ideas provide the logical foundation for the complex subject of the meeting. They cover beliefs and attitudes, as well as practices and procedures:

* Joint effort is a powerful dimension.
* The trick is relating, not winning.
* Leaders vary in the degree of authority granted them.
* Number and mix of participants are important.
* Consensus at one end—railroading on the other.
* The more rigorous the requirements, the better members perform.
* Flexibility is required to shape the meeting to its particular goal.

2. A <u>centered</u> meeting brushes away obstacles and distractions from the task while providing ground rules and techniques which lead directly to the goal.

4:
What Kind of Leader Are You?

The Three Types of Leaders

Studies by Lewin, Lippit and R. White of many different organizations reveal three broad categories of leaders, each with a different method and each with different degrees of success:

* The "laissez-faire" leader
* The "I'm in command here" leader
* The "I believe in people" leader

Laissez-faire. A leader with a laissez-faire attitude does not last long. Such a leader wants a meeting to run itself. If you ask the laissez-faire leader why he or she acts in this way, the answer you often get is: "Giving people plenty of rope brings out the best in them." Deeper probing often reveals a person who really doesn't want to lead. Since such talents don't belong in front of a conference room or at the head of a conference table, they are quickly replaced.

You can recognize a laissez-faire leader by his or her low energy and frequent absence. After calling a meeting together, these leaders frequently find themselves occupied with activities of "higher priority." They may cancel the meeting at the last moment or make a token appearance, turn the chair over to someone else, or leave the room. The only greater discomfort than watching your leader disinterestedly leave the meeting is to have to take over the chair yourself! The implication is too obvious: "This meeting is OK for people who have nothing better to do; your leader has been called to higher service."

Individual energies and group energies must be channeled to be used well. Without effective leadership, the meeting degenerates into general frustration, anger and chaos.

Scratch the laissez-faire attitude from your list of useful types of leadership.

I'm in command here. Depending on his or her organizational clout, the I'm-in-command leader can be shockingly successful as an individual. However, the effect on the organization is quite another matter. Tough I'm-in-command leaders hold such a tight rein on the members that soon they have a roomful of puppets. Each member eagerly (pitifully) says to the leader: "I'm not sure what you want, boss, but you can count on me to do whatever you want and whenever you want it, without questions."

When an authoritarian leader runs a meeting, only one person speaks at a time—and only when called upon. No spontaneity here! The leader plans, directs and draws out the responses he or she wants. The leader makes certain that previously established goals are met—and met quickly. The meeting is steered from problem to problem, and each problem is "solved"—even if the decisions are based on incomplete or absent information, even if better solutions are available but not mentioned because everyone's discouraged from speaking up. Matters that require prompt attention never surface—until long after the meeting is over, when too little time may be available to develop rational solutions. At that point the I'm-in-command leader moans about the "lack of talent they give me to work with! How can I do everything myself?"

The effects of this kind of leadership on employee performance are devastating. The short-run advantage of apparent success in meeting objectives soon is overshadowed by a demoralized organization, unable to think for itself. No meetings at all are better than such meetings.

If such leadership is encouraged within an organization, you can bet that any new leaders who eventually make their way to positions of authority will behave in the same way. If kill-or-be-killed is the only way to survive, look for other employment, keep quiet, learn the game, and stay on Valium until your turn comes to proclaim, "I'm in command here!" That is, if your organization stays alive long enough for you to advance.

I believe in people. This type of leader takes the biggest risks and achieves the greatest leadership successes. This leader sees people as seeking responsibility and capable of achieving high degrees of self-direction, ingenuity and creativity. The strategy is: *"Remain flexible and adaptable."* Such a leader has thought seriously about the job of leadership and about the qualities people can cultivate.

For example, Bill Sandman, an I-believe-in-people leader, has been hard-headed but sensitive as he has worked his way up through one of the largest corporations in the United States. He is now executive vice-president and appears headed for the top of the executive ladder. Recently he was asked to define a good leader.

I started out in the personnel department of this company 12 years ago. My training was nonexistent, since I majored in English in college and our company is a leader in the aerospace industry. Once I got my job, I began to take night courses in engineering so I would be able to understand the jobs for which our department was supplying bodies. Then I began to do some graduate work in management and behavioral science and got a master's degree.

My big break came when I developed a management recruitment program for our company as part of my master's thesis. I submitted it to my boss, who thought enough of it to send it "upstairs." After the program was adopted and launched by my company, I was promoted. In two years I became vice-president of executive development—a minor vice-presidency, you can be sure—but a boost, all the same.

One thing followed another, and now I find myself attending meeting after meeting, and most of the time I am the chairman of the meeting. I tell you all this because I want you to understand how I came to my present thinking.

The leader of a meeting does things differently from other types of leaders. A military man, a Little League manager, the head of a college English department, all have different requirements for success in running a meeting. Even an executive of a large organization is not automatically qualified to run a meeting.

I like to use my knowledge and my skills not only to meet the goal of a meeting—the final product—but also to understand how we get there. By that I mean learning how people work together, what knowledge they give each other and the make-up of a successful team. If we don't pay attention to these factors, we lose valuable insights into what people need to feel satisfied and productive and into how we should manage people in situations other than meetings. If we don't stop to find out such things, a lot of valuable information goes down the drain.

My aim is to develop a mature working team while we're on our way to a goal. This makes meetings a living-learning-working experience instead of a prison sentence.

I look for such things as the following:

- *clear and direct communication*
- *focused goals and purposes*
- *shared responsibilities*
- *full use of the many different abilities of the team members*
- *self-correction of fatigue and tension within the members*
- *healthy balance between cooperation and competition*
- *appropriate harnessing of feelings and thoughts*
- *full expression of ideas and insights*

As I look at people arriving for a meeting, I see a rich stew of resources—each member adding a special background and capability to the meeting that is about to begin. I also see a widely varied group of temperaments ranging from lively to phlegmatic, from detail-occupied to imaginative. My job, as leader, is to make it possible for every member to make a full contribution. And I know that each member arrives with a purpose in mind. The ones whom I have worked with before know that they will be given a chance to make a contribution, and I like to think that they're eager to do so. The ones who are new to me may wonder how they can hide during the meeting. Of course, there are always those who are ready to contribute no matter how new they are to a situation.

A leader of this caliber, then, sees the role of leader as acting as a catalyst for the meeting itself and for the many other activities of the organization. The members under this kind of leadership find that their work days fill important needs in their lives.

In the following hypothetical illustration, observe how the three different leaders run the same meeting.

A citizens group held a one-day conference on approaches to energy conservation at individual, corporate and governmental levels. The goal was to make recommendations to national legislative representatives. Those attending included men and women from business, industry and government. They were economists, engineers, biologists and consumers. The theme was designed for maximum interest and effort: "Our Resources: Use, Waste, Save, Develop."

Laissez-faire. Barry was picked by the citizens group to run the meeting because he was known for being at ease with many different kinds of people. He placed complete trust in the ability of people to "use freedom of speech and thought profitably." How? "By leaving them alone." He believed a meeting needed no guidance. Mainly, he participated by sitting on the side with a satisfied look, enjoying what he called "a completely free exchange of ideas."

Barry didn't remind members to keep the theme and their relationship to it in sight at all times. As a result, everyone repeated the same point of view held from the past. There were a few unsuccessful attempts by some to try to work together but there was no leader to cement the mix. Barry provided neither a focus nor a goal.

The biologist and engineer seemed to enjoy the freewheeling and even unruly spirit. Lester and Nick became fast friends, chatting and getting to know each other during the meeting. Once, Nick stood up and made an impassioned speech about the need for energy conservation. Laura, the legislator, said, "I agree with you. You're absolutely right. But I assume we all feel that way or we wouldn't be here. Now, what proposals have you to suggest?" Nick shrugged, Lester laughed, no one volunteered an idea and the meeting turned into a shouting free-for-all. Laura scowled and whispered to the next person that this reminded her more of lobbyists in Washington than of a group trying to address itself in a balanced way to a problem of national survival.

A few, undaunted by a lack of structure, continued to try to mobilize a group effort. Others sat on their haunches, feeling vaguely resentful of a leader who let everyone do what they felt like but who failed in a fundamental sense. Very little progress was achieved in developing a plan for the saving and spending of resources.

I'm in command here. Jeannie convinced the citizens group that, since she'd organized the conference, she'd be well suited to running the meeting.

Jeannie prepared an advance plan to make sure that the meeting would run according to set procedures. For example, she insisted that each representative give a brief account of his or her view of conservation. Then, after summarizing these reports, she called on members to comment on the different views.

Clearly, Jeannie believed in participation—but participation under her specific direction. Every time the conversation began to flow freely, she stepped on the brake and structured the life out of the discussion.

Before long, the stronger members tried to rebel against her in subtle ways. Unfortunately, this type of leader has a grip of iron.

Edgar, an economist and a highly independent person, tried to break away from the script prepared by the one "in command." He gave a humorous account of how certain people in his community defined conservation. "To them, conservation means turning off the bathroom light when you leave the room." Just as Edgar was about to apply this example to a proposal for educating the public about conservation, Jeannie interrupted. "I think you should stick to your own field. Now, have you anything to say about the economics of conservation? If not, please sit down."

The I'm-in-command leader abuses the theme of the meeting by treating it mechanically and as a medium for controlling the members. The results were as you'd expect. Those who conformed, marched in file and delivered the words Jeannie wanted to hear. The "free souls" who didn't like the idea of being ordered about dissipated much of their energy in opposition.

I believe in people. Max was always considered to be a valuable member at previous meetings of the citizens group—mainly because of his versatility. His words were listened to, yet he never stepped on toes. In this respect he was a model member: he wasn't looking for glory and he found pleasure in teamwork. When this conference was proposed, he was the first choice of the citizens group to be the leader.

He took the theme seriously: "Our Resources: Use, Waste, Save, Develop." This democratic leader realized the practical importance of having representatives generating their ideas, attitudes, experiences and feelings about the subject freely. This could provide an excellent base for writing a joint report reflecting understanding and compromise.

The sincerity encouraged by the way the meeting was run led to a stimulating candidness. Roger, the industrialist, admitted that, "I really do lay awake nights wondering whether 'farming' lumber on my company's 4 million acres of property really maintains the ecological balance." Nadine, a consumer representative, admitted that she was prejudiced about truckers "who waste gasoline by driving too fast," even though she knew sometimes it meant the difference between staying in or going out of business.

This was no doubt a productive meeting because the leader's "volume" was modulated to make things happen and to let things happen. This conference became the first of a series of annual meetings, funded by a private grant, providing a steady stream of useful reports for legislative action.

Hopefully, by now you're acquiring the belief that people can work well together when the conditions are right. And you, as leader or as member, are beginning to know how to make those conditions right. There's more to believe and learn, however. So, continue with your journey!

Style

Style in leading includes almost everything that has to do with how you conduct a meeting. Style is fixed since it is based on unchanging and relatively inaccessible attitudes in your inner life. Psychologists tell us that reflections from our inner self may be seen in styles of walking, handwriting, playing, working—and leading a meeting!

Your style as a leader may be anything from retiring to charismatic, from despotic to inactively non-controlling, from self-doubting to self-acclaiming. But the key to using your unique style successfully is to adapt it to the principles of good leading.

For example, Edward Metcalf has a negative and gruff manner of leading. Inwardly, he is very sensitive to the opinions of others and needs their approval. This comes out at meetings in such remarks as, "I know you don't think much of my ideas, but I don't care. I'm going to make my suggestion and cram it down your throats, if I have to!"

Such behavior actually can be recycled to a firm down-to-business manner which would earn Metcalf the respect and approval he wants and needs. Metcalf can learn to "play down" the negative aspects of his style and adapt a more positive and democratic approach: "I'd like to propose a plan and then get your feedback on it. I hope you find it workable, but if it's not popular, I assure you, I'm *not* going to cram it down your throats."

What you should aim for is a harmony between your inner self and the outer part of you. As a leader of 11 years of experience expressed it: "I'm at my peak when I'm being myself while succeeding as a leader."

In the guide below, we invite you to check some major sources of your behavioral style suggested by the work of Karen Horney. There are three basic categories: Moving Toward, Moving Against and Moving Away From. Following is a personal analysis made by a leader from each category. After you read their self-descriptions, study the examples of good and wasteful leading styles. Since there are no "pure" style-types, find your own best combination and let it direct you toward a skilled and effective performance as a caring and democratic leader.

Moving Toward

I believe I am sociable, warm and tactful. I try to be open with lots of people and I think they like my candidness as well as my patience. People call on me for favors. I like to be helpful and I don't mind going out of my way for someone with a problem. While I can concentrate and work alone when I have to, I guess I prefer working with others: at home, at a party or at a meeting. To me, nothing can beat the sense of elation when you team up—whether it be with one person or 20—and roll up your sleeves and dig in together. Sure, sometimes you get into arguments. Sure, sometimes you get frustrated. But the working it out and getting back on an even keel is half the fun! I guess I'd have to say that I owe people a lot; they've helped me to get to know myself pretty well.

Good Leading Style: (1) Has confidence in the give-and-take ability of members. Communicates openly and clearly because of a willingness to know and to be known. Serves as a model of self-acceptance. All this adds up to a high degree of enthusiasm and alertness. (2) Invites differences among members by encouraging expression of their deepest, most individual and creative ideas as a source of energy for getting things done. (3) Helpfulness is translated into practical and tangible actions for giving members needed support and recognition.

Wasteful Leading Style: (1) Movement toward people becomes a "sugary" end in itself, leaving no room for a healthy, "salty" clash of opinions and personalities. Undue emphasis on compliance and consensus gives the discussion a flavor of sweet taffy. Too much stress on team togetherness overshadows individuals and the task. Result is a pleasant, congenial team which agrees on everything but really doesn't tackle the job. (2) Leader guards against criticism by leaning over backward to please. (3) The boundary between leader and member becomes blurred. Time is wasted when members have to fill in the leadership vacuum.

Moving Against

I make sure that I stay on top of every situation. If I don't, people will take advantage, of that I am sure. My attitude is: I'll take care of myself and you take care of yourself; just don't step on my toes. Nothing is really worthwhile or enjoyable unless you fight hard for it. No one hands you anything on a silver platter. So I've learned you have to figure out what you want and how to go after it. The trouble is, someone is always trying to prevent you from getting where you want to go. That's why it's always a 15-rounder. Frankly, I get tired and lonely sometimes. I'd like to get closer to people, but I can't let down my guard in the "ring." So I do anything necessary to win and if my humanity suffers, if I lack friends and closeness, well that's a price I guess I have to pay.

Good Leading Style: (1) Has developed so much of his own ambition and sense of power that meeting members get swept up in his tornado of energy. The atmosphere is like that of a coach and team before the big game. (2) Members with aggressive and combative tendencies are subtly rewarded. (3) Although the energies released are rather one-sided, there is an effective trend toward meeting the goal—getting the job done. This leader serves as a model of commitment because of his awe and submission to the organization's pressures and demands on meeting members.

Wasteful Leading Style: (1) Will do anything to maintain competition, often by setting one against the other, then stepping in to "resolve" the situation by taking over with his own plan. (2) Often puts forth a disarming kind of cordiality. This keeps the members at a low boil of anger and disappointment. They use up energy in subtly resisting the manipulation. (3) Is so vulnerable when challenged that independent opinions are made to appear unreasonable and unpopular. Some members are crushed by the blast of this leader's belligerent manner.

Moving Away From

I find myself looking in at a meeting from the outside, even though I'm present. Not that I dislike people. I am a distant admirer. I care deeply for what I do but the kind of work I prefer seems to be with things and ideas, not people.

Why others do not listen to me as much as I would hope is difficult to understand. I guess my delivery is dry. Still, I have a lot of interesting ideas and feelings which stay locked up. I am practical and realistic in many small ways but when it comes to an overall grasp of what's going on in a group of people, I easily miss the boat. I suppose pulling away from others gives me blind spots in being able to know what makes them tick.

Good Leading Style: (1) Has a flair for logic and mastery of small detail, to good advantage. The thinking level of the meeting is raised as members reflect and deliberate more effectively in keeping with the leader's example. (2) Even though he avoids contacts this leader welcomes the actions of warmer and better connected members. Logically, he realizes that they provide what he lacks. (3) Feels secure enough with his own rational strengths to welcome the initiative and creativity of members.

Wasteful Leading Style: (1) The loneliness in being removed from others has left a cold and bitter core. Leads with a cold and grim spirit. (2) Does things in a mechanical way. Any sign of closeness or involvement is seen as dangerous. (3) Goes through the motions of getting opinions and ideas but the meeting doesn't take root. Standing some distance away from the closest participant, this basically shy leader seems to be in slight haze.

A case illustration will show how these leaders with three specific patterns of feelings toward people, conduct their meetings.

Let's suppose all three leaders (Toward, Against and Away From) are confronted with the situation below. Each handles it in a typical way, quite differently from the others. The setting is a well-established advertising agency at a business crossroads. They have to look outside the city for accounts because several large corporations they represented pulled up stakes to relocate in other parts of the country. A suggested substitute market is a rural area in a 200-mile radius of the city.

However, few salespeople in the agency have enthusiasm for making rural contacts. It just seems so unfamiliar and distant a prospect. And it is felt that the potential clients don't care to deal with this "big city" agency. A meeting is called to examine the problem of whether the company realistically could approach the new market, given all the doubts that were expressed.

The Moving Toward Leader. Melody Velasquez is a respected assistant to the president of the advertising company. Usually she supervises public relations but this time, as a special assignment, she's asked to call a meeting of agency personnel and sales managers. She has the reputation of being warm and accessible. People are often seen trudging into her office with one burden or another, and emerging with a lighter step.

At the meeting, Melody asks each member to pair up with someone seated nearby. She gives instructions to the "couples" to "Come up with one objection to the agency moving into rural territory, and a possible answer to this objection." Melody, herself, joins in as a member of one of the couples. The results are then shared with the group as a whole. As a consequence, members feel supported and understood by each other as they recognize common worries—as well as solutions. The tide turns in the direction of "pooling our resources to go after that market as a team." The meeting ends on that note.

The Moving Against Leader. Pug Wilkins was brought into the company recently because of his aggressiveness—even combativeness—in getting people to do what he wanted. In the company, he makes a practice of asking for suggestions, mulling them over and then rejecting them.

At the meeting, every time someone reasons against the plan of moving into the unknown territory, Wilkins sends an annoyed glance in their direction. "There is no place for 'urban specialists' in this company!" he announces angrily.

Then, with malicious glee, he invites everyone into the fray.

"Will someone sit here opposite me and take the part of the editor of the *Rural Times*, a representative newspaper of the new territory? I'll take the part of one of our salespeople." J. Murray nervously agrees to "play" editor. In his role of salesperson, Wilkins argues aggressively.

"Don't be a jerk, Murray. Just because we're a city agency doesn't mean we can't relate to a rural account. We service all our clients equally and if you ran your newspaper even half as impartially, maybe I'd consider reading it. Right now, I just stuff it in the garbage pail!"

The dialogue, with its belligerent tone, nonetheless strikes some sparks of truth about the agency's capacity to handle the new kind of assignment. Murray, somewhat browbeaten, is more or less convinced.

Moving Away From Leader. Horace Heidt is known as having thought up some of the best advertising campaigns in the company's history—all in the privacy of his own office. Brilliant as an idea man, Horace rarely comes down from his "ivory tower" of ideas. Fortunately, he has an amiable secretary who serves as an intermediary between "Invisible Horace" and the others.

At the meeting, Horace, who is leading, arrives with a package of index cards. "What are those, Horace?" someone asks. He has aroused curiosity. "Well, on these cards is my analysis of the nature of the 10 chief business organizations in the new territory." He passes out the cards and says no more. Everyone studies the cards. There has been doubt about the possibility of expansion, but now the cards stimulate a lively discussion. Horace has little to say to anyone directly, but everyone else participates in the pros and cons of a rural vs. urban market. By the end of the meeting, this detached and logical approach—based mainly on providing information—succeeds in giving members the assurance needed to overcome strong doubts about going ahead with the new territory.

Basic Moves

Can all group-leading behavior be broken down into specific categories? Dr. Morton A. Lieberman, in his *Behavior and Impact of Leaders*, showed not only that the answer is "yes," but that there are five separate categories. His study lists all the major characteristics or actions of the leader. How do you function within these five basic actions?

1. **Evocative.** Designed to get members to respond by bringing them out.
2. **Coherence-making.** Aims at improving content, logic and clarity of the subject matter of the meeting.
3. **Support.** Used to give members the essential approval and acceptance needed to avoid tension.
4. **Managing behavior.** Aims at getting individuals to work better for their own—or team—development.
5. **Use of self.** Involves self-stating and modeling by leader.

Consider the first characteristic, *Evocative*, and see how it works for you. If you tend to shy away from controlling the meeting ("laissez-faire") while also favoring closer human contacts ("moving toward"), you won't be involved in actively trying to get people to respond. Rather, your preference for sociability *indirectly* will evoke the response of members.

It is time for you to embark on a search for your own natural style and how it can adapt to the principles of good leading.

In the following chart the leader is rated as: *I'm In Command* (tending toward democratic) and *Moving Toward* (but not strongly so).

According to the ratings on these two scales, the leader carries out the five basic moves in these ways:

1. **Evocative.** Offers a friendly but firm invitation to a member to answer a question.

2. **Coherence-making.** Gives directions about the next logical steps to be considered, while glancing at one of the members present, sitting directly opposite.

3. **Support.** Makes a suggestion about trusting the leader's judgment with the aim of bolstering members' confidence in the progress of the meeting.

4. **Managing behavior.** Reminds members that, as representative of the company, the leader is responsible for team development. Members are told to ask any questions about how this may be accomplished. Their processes are observed and suggestions are made for improvement.

5. Use of self. Leader cites personal experience to illuminate a situation in which it was necessary to oppose regulations of an outside agency. The leader uses this example to encourage a member to be assertive.

SEE WHERE YOU FIT ON THESE SCALES AND HOW YOU WOULD CARRY OUT THE BASIC MOVES. ARE YOU SATISFIED? DO YOU WANT TO CHANGE IN A DIRECTION TO MAKE YOU MORE EFFECTIVE?

LEADING WITH SKILL AND STYLE

Where Do You Stand?
Scale of Person-to-Person Contact

		Moving toward	Moving away from	Moving against
Scale of Controlling	Laissez-faire			
	I Believe In People			
	I'm In Command	●		

MEMO

SUBJECT: Leading with both skill and style.

1. Leaders can be described by the kind of control they exercise, as well as by their style.

2. The best leader has specific, identifiable skills and characteristics that increase productivity.

3. A knowledge of the three basic models helps leaders analyze their own natural assets and preferences and proceed according to these guiding questions:

* What is your preferred way of encouraging a team effort?
* What is there in your personal manner which can build confidence, increase self-respect and help fulfill aspirations of team members?
* What is there about you which interferes with good leading and which must be soft-pedalled?
* How can you shape the five basic moves—seen in all team-leading—to correspond with your own tendencies?

5:
In the Beginning

Meetings are essential to the proper functioning of any organization—even a mom-and-pop grocery store. Mom and pop, too, have to meet and discuss how their interactions as partners can be made more effective. In a large organization, meetings make the difference between success and failure. Industry, commerce, government, foundations, universities—all structures that have a serious purpose and must get work done on time—depend on meetings to bring key people together and make effective use of their time and energy. How else can they bring out the strengths, ideas and visions of their best people? How else can they move steadily toward their organizational goals?

Experienced leaders know that meetings can generate a collective energy that is far greater than the sum of individual energy. They know that well-run meetings charge up those who attend, making them eager to contribute. They know that at successful meetings, everyone focuses on the task at hand, and helps each other open up to make maximum contributions. These leaders know that they play an important part in ensuring positive attitudes and receptivity.

Here is how a leader can "set the stage."

Problem-Facing

Be aware of the common human tendency to avoid seeing and discussing problems. Members find it safer to avoid—than to confront—what's wrong with the workings of a meeting. And they will resist recognizing and bringing up important problems associated with the topic under discussion. No one wants to "rock the boat." Which is where you come in! Your skill as a leader depends on your ability to encourage sensitivity to problems, assertiveness in tagging them and ingenuity in encouraging their expression.

Advance Planning

Advance planning allows you to center the task and anticipate obstacles, as well as to map out the best format. Serving in the role of *host* to the members is crucial to the spirit of a meeting. Also, an *informal contract* must be drawn up, explained and accepted. Only when the stage is set can you feel confident that your well-intentioned plans and techniques are on firm ground.

Involve members actively in advance planning by asking them to participate, even in advance of the meeting. In a verbal or written memo, suggest: "Can you drop by on Monday between 10 and 12 o'clock to help plan for the meeting?"

When circumstances don't allow for any prior discussion, the first few minutes of a meeting can be used to review the agenda for its precise relevance to each member and to establish realistic goals.

A written plan of the meeting, prepared in advance with the aid of several members, serves to activate the skills of planning and initiative. The resulting transfer of part of the "ownership" of the meeting to members produces commitment and involvement.

Robert Benson is the vice-president of Silver Lode, Inc., a large engineering firm. His management style combines the qualities of the precise engineer with his intuitive knowledge of people. He's successful at using this sensitivity about things and people in leading a meeting.

Silver Lode's president is chafing at the bit. An important contract was delayed, apparently by being bounced around from one office to the next. There is a danger that a competing firm will step in. The president asks Benson to get the matter resolved. Benson asks several of his staff to help in the advance planning. Since he wanted a broad sampling of opinion, he invited several members who had expertise with the issue and who would be affected by the outcome.

Plan of Meeting

Date, Time, Place: September 5th, 2:00–3:30, Conference Room

Attending: (From Programming) Joe, Bart, Alex
(From Contracts) Phyllis, Herb, Sam
(From Purchasing) Susan, Walt
(Vice-president and chairing the meeting) Benson

General Problem: A client on a large contract filled out the lengthy forms and specs we require before we bid. Some of us are bothered that the client was unclear in expressing certain details. Some of us feel it is necessary to go back to our client for further clarification. Others among us want to leave well enough alone and are prepared to go ahead with our final bid.

Type of Meeting: Problem-solving and Decision-making.

The Goal: To get an accurate judgment about how much more information is really needed, measured against the risk of delay. While pressing our client for more information, other bidders may take away the contract. The desired outcome: Members will arrive at a consensus today. Failing this, Benson will make the decision.

Specific Approach or Emphasis: To hear out the differing positions on standards of contract-writing and bidding. Further, to weigh these positions against the needs of the organization.

Bugs and Obstacles Anticipated: Both sides of the question—caution and enterprise—are persuasive. The pitfall is that members become less rational about advancing a view that simply *feels* better to them.

Benson's meeting goes well. The two opposing points of view are presented and better understood. One side is characterized by Susan, a valuable member of the organization who feels immobilized by not having complete information from the client. Sam and others, on the other side, are impatient to accept the client's report, arguing that, "Whatever we don't know now, we can get later."

With further open discussion, members begin to realize how their own personal interpretations of the situation serve to advance or block the needs of the organization and client. As a result of a fuller review of facts and attitudes, Susan no longer insists on her personal preference. Sam finds a way of expressing his point of view, without pressing or flaunting it. Once issues like these become clear, the decision falls into place. The bid is submitted that afternoon.

The Host

The leader is in the position of a host greeting guests. First impressions can impart a warm glow, be neutral or leave the guests with cold or unpleasant memories of being excluded.

Here are some old and new recipes for getting things rolling as the meeting starts:

- Arrive a few minutes early to make sure that there are enough seats. They should not be arranged in rows, theatre style, or you'll have a meeting of spectators, not participants.
- Mingle informally, or at least exchange friendly glances before the meeting starts. This is a good way to show your readiness to come together in the same team.
- As you start the meeting, relieve any mystery surrounding unknown participants. Introduce members new to the group, and those who are known but who may be making an unexpected appearance because of their special contributions. If an outside visitor is present, explain why he or she is there. All this will put everyone on the same starting line.
- Ask if anyone can serve as note-taker for outlines and final summaries. Members will decide whether they want to rotate the job in the middle of the meeting, or not have written notes at all.
- If you have any announcements not related to the central task, get them over with quickly. Don't let this drain time from the main job.
- A latecomer should neither be rewarded nor punished, but motioned to a seat. Don't stop the meeting in its tracks to bring him/her up to date (reward). And don't let him/her search and struggle for a seat (punishment).

By now you know that people think best when under the least strain. Members arriving at a meeting are ill at ease and tense, covering this up under the guise of small talk and other common props. They did not choose the time, place or format of the meeting, but were instructed to go. They left the comfortable isolation of their offices, the relative freedom of their movements in the field or the coziness of familiar working conditions. They were asked to enter a relatively unknown territory. They are plunged into an hour or more of a new set of problems and circumstances.

The purely physical arrangements including seats, air and light, range from relaxing to irritating. Some people are oblivious to extremes of light and temperature, while others cease to function. Chairs for meetings which last longer than a half-hour should be reasonably comfortable. If you have the choice, wooden rocking chairs are preferable. They keep people in one spot while releasing body tensions and accommodating shifts of position. Seating is best arranged in a circle or semicircle so that everyone can see and hear everyone else. Seating in rows is designed for spectators, for rigid audience control and for a study of the backs of necks!

Stimulating or soothing beverages served in the back of the meeting room can refresh people when they begin to feel drained. (On the other hand, don't create a party atmosphere or you may give the members a misleading sense of escape from the rigors of meeting. And they may not be able to return.)

A Contract with Large Letters

How to act, what to say and what ground rules to follow at meetings are often left vague, unspoken or abandoned to chance. With a contract, everyone understands the guidelines. It gives you opportunities for greater freedom and control of action. Without it, "playing it safe" becomes the name of the game.

There are certain contracts, however, which aren't suitable for our kinds of meetings where members are pulling together for a common goal. One is the formal "rules of order," which applies to large—or potentially unruly—gatherings, such as legislative sessions. At the opposite end, a contract which loosely invites people to be "themselves" does not give the necessary kind of intellectual structure required for work goals.

The most productive ground rules encourage participation and democracy, rather than exploitation and paternalism. In a paternalistic situation, the norms of a meeting reflect fears of punishment, minimal feelings of responsibility and reluctance to cooperate.

Legal pacts for behavior at meetings are never in writing, but if they were, the contract below is the one which we favor. It provides a safe and navigable channel.

CONTRACT

BETWEEN the parties known as LEADER and MEMBERS.

The terms of this AGREEMENT preserve the rights of individual expression while safeguarding team effort.

The LEADER agrees:

1. I will be fair and open-minded.
2. I believe each person's skills can be tapped.
3. I encourage each participant to assist the leader—when possible—as catalyst, coordinator and conductor.
4. I aim to express myself clearly and directly.
5. I will defend members against unfair attacks.

The MEMBER agrees:

1. I join the task and keep it centered.
2. I accept the leader as guardian of the meeting and of our method.
3. I can speak for myself only.
4. I give and get what I want.
5. Distractions have special priorities in being heard and announced.
6. I am responsible for myself and will not wait to be called on.
7. I will be prepared to sum up and evaluate so that the conclusions do not remain up in the air or ambiguous.

SIGNATURES

The following is a way of putting into words the above contract of a *centered* meeting. A *centered* leader gets things done by giving the person and the task equal importance.

The Leader Levels. The first part of the contract is a statement of attitude by the leader. He/she levels with, and orients members to, certain standards. (The wording can be changed to fit the situation.)

Our organization brings us together as a team to study this problem or situation. We are told to come up with the best and most efficient solution and a plan to expedite it.

I happen to be leading because of my experience and know-how in running a meeting. (Or I may know more about the background or facts of the task than most others here.) Beyond that, each of you is an expert in some way in listening, talking, thinking and in understanding people.

Each of you can try to be a catalyst, coordinator and conductor. You will not be stepping on my toes if you help maintain the flow and energy. This means paying attention to how the meeting is going, not just how you are going. My meeting, your meeting, our meeting—one cannot succeed without the other.

I hope to let you see clearly into what I say and do—to part the velvet curtain which only muffles communication between member and leader. I will speak for myself and hope you will, too. I shall stand by any member who is under unfair attack. I shall free the team when it's shackled by the actions of one member.

You can harvest and use your human resources, not waste them, by adhering to and respecting the following ground rules.

Ground Rules for a Centered Meeting. Members' nagging doubts are calmed at a *centered* meeting. Yes, the leader really says that his/her aim is fairness, openness and encouragement. No hidden agenda, alliances, pre-packaged solutions. Members feel ready to get started. Good working conditions have been established.

Now the leader can mention: "The teeth of the contract, the ground rules, will be brought in, one by one, as the need arises in the early part of this meeting. The ground rules may be questioned or modified, if there are strong reasons to do so." But the leader explains that, in their present form, they have proven effective.

Here is the substance of the seven ground rules:

1. The team has a task for the meeting.

The task for each member is to relate specific thoughts, feelings and actions to the theme. (The task must be kept centered.)

2. There is always a team leader.

The task of the team leader is to be chief guardian of the contract by serving as a model participant and a liaison with the organization.

3. Members represent only themselves.

Often, a member generalizes (i.e., "People always say this, or that") or speaks for the others with a "we" or "you" statement. This disguises the speaker's own judgments and feelings. The shortest distance between speaker and hearer is an "I" statement.

4. Everyone must give and get from each meeting exactly what he or she wants to give and get.

This rule asks each person to weigh his/her contribution on the scale of what is best for the group effort without stifling valid differences of opinion.

5. Nothing that anyone wants to say or do—ideas, suggestions, feelings—is ruled out until it is heard out.

Often, these departures and distractions represent lively and alternate views of the task. Once a member is distracted, there is no better way to bring him back than to tolerate a brief airing of an off-center comment.

6. Everyone is responsible for his/her own participation.

This counters the lifelong injunction of waiting to be called on. Leader and members are given the freedom to find their own style and contribute accordingly.

7. Every meeting must end with a clear statement of what was accomplished, what remains to be done—and when.

Putting together different views and conclusions of the same event is a valuable exercise in communication. It also leaves everyone with approximately the same conclusion about follow-up steps.

These ground rules discourage members from using meetings in self-centered ways as sanctuaries, theaters-in-the-round or battlegrounds. Instead, the contract requires members to pay equal attention to self, others and the task. As a result, they discover a way to become more involved productively on a team.

IN THE BEGINNING 57

At a recent training session for sales managers, several objections were raised about the "overexposure" caused by the ground rules. The leader, Martha Knowles, answered: "If the ground rules carry some risk, they produce higher dividends." Martha pointed out that no one is forced to abide by every rule, but rather, to aim *at* them.

"Do we ever stop observing, sizing up and trying to form impressions of others? In the first few moments of any encounter, we are already 'exposed,'" Martha continued. "The trouble is, you and I can't even get the benefit of this exposure unless someone tells us a bit about ourselves. If I ask for some feedback about me, and you give me some constructive impressions, does this make me any more exposed? Of course not. It puts me more in touch with myself and gives me more power and self-control as a leader."

A good contract gives you the choice:

♦ By *not following* its ground rules, you, as leader or member, can make meetings dull and unproductive, sapping the strength and ideas of the people who attend.
♦ By *following* its ground rules, you, as leader or member, can play a vital role in energizing yourself and others, increasing productivity and encouraging the flow of ideas.

Making Each Phase Count

The most productive meetings go through certain normal phases, each serving as a foundation for the next. This is true whether a meeting is a one-time, one-hour session, a longer period or even several sessions. The leader identifies—and in fact, introduces—these gradually emerging stages. This enables members to suit their actions and goals to the situation. There are four such "changes of scenery."

1. Before a meeting, the leader asks participants to assist in planning and taking more responsibility for the meeting. There are questions of size of meeting, composition and duration which need answers. Members can also help define and word the task as outlined in this chapter in the Advance Plan of Meeting (page 50).

2. As the meeting starts, alert members go on "reconnaissance," surveying the specific styles and personalities of others, and making tentative judgments about the best procedures. You're faced with the uncertainty of exploring new situations. You can get your bearings by asking yourself: "How can I use my knowledge of the facts and subject matter of this meeting, while relating to the team members? What are the ground rules of behavior?"

3. In the main part of the meeting, the task is defined and developed. Various opinions, assessments and interpretations are given and received about each other's contributions. In this stage where the footwork is steadier, cooperation and coordination are possible.

4. On the last lap, the integration of each person's efforts is seen. The result is a solution which has the stamp of both individual and team effort. It's here that members agree more readily on the final form of the decision. They feel free to give active support and approval to each other.

MEMO

SUBJECT: How to get off to a good start.

1. A good leader sets the atmosphere and ground rules of the meeting that tap, rather than stifle, the motivations and resources of those in attendance.

2. Members involved in advance planning develop a feeling of being more in control. Also, by asking members to share in advance planning, the leader succeeds in transferring some of the ownership to them.

3. Serving as host, the wise leader realizes people think best <u>when not under strain.</u>

4. The contract brings everyone together in an active partnership where ideas flow freely into common channels, but where individuals are respected for their unique contributions.

5. The phases of a meeting are unfolded by the leader, providing a firm basis for each succeeding change of scenery.

6:
The Leader Takes Hold

Now you're ready to take the raw product—the problem or agenda—and process it through the complicated meeting machinery. The task has to be guided at every step, beginning with the question, "What is the problem?" and ending with "How do we apply the solution?"

From Task to Theme

From the outset it's you, the leader, who determines the extent to which the task needs to be analyzed, polished or developed. Where routine working group assignments are involved, the tasks performed by teams, units or committees do not require much exploring, probing or other special teamwork. The task is done by simply stringing together the efforts of those present.

At such a meeting the assignment need not carry any more than a simple statement of what has to be done. For example: "Getting Acquainted with the New System of Record-Keeping." Members will learn about the new method of record-keeping in their own ways by listening, absorbing and asking questions. This kind of meeting is carried out routinely.

Where more than routine assignments are involved, the agenda can be stated in a way to get the meeting started on the right foot. Carson, a vice-president of sales, had the problem of lagging sales over the last two years. He knew that the problem was deeper than a matter of production schedules or sales ability. He realized that this problem lent itself to broader dimensions and richer solutions. He decided to develop this task into a more productive "theme." First, he had to provide members with a springboard for their thoughts, feelings and interactions by wording the task accordingly.

With this in mind, Carson converted the topic—which had to do with lagging sales—to a task-theme. He called it "Keeping Up, Falling Behind or Getting Ahead." In offering this kind of *centering*, he developed the task into a broader theme.

Then he gave members a chance to think about their personal reactions to this theme. As a result, a number of stimulating ideas were generated and used profitably throughout the rest of the meeting:

* What does "getting ahead" mean for me in this company?
* What kind of pressure is good for me or bad for me?
* Am I finding it more difficult in the field but failing to get help from management?
* Have I been pushing hard but in the wrong direction?
* Am I *just* "keeping up" because of loss of faith in the product?

Dealing with the task in this way has the special advantage of opening it up to input at various levels. There are many specific advantages to *centering* the task and formulating the theme.

1. The member becomes more involved and committed.
2. The task develops a deeper meaning.
3. The theme serves as a beacon, a promising goal.
4. There is a forward thrust suggested by "getting ahead" rather than "dipping sales."
5. The task has more elbow-room, and lends itself to open-ended interpretations.

By now you know the importance of properly wording the underlying theme. Here are some suggestions to guide you in formulating tasks with the added power of themes.

- Bring in the member's attitudes, opinions and relationships to the task.
- Suggest the use of teamwork.
- Make it open-ended.
- Give it a positive thrust.

This kind of *centering* of a meeting, by recognizing underlying themes, may be done at any one of these stages:

Pre-meeting: When planning for the meeting, think of how to word the task in ways we have suggested.

Announcement of Agenda: When the meeting starts, if the task lends itself to a broader treatment, it can be stated according to the suggested guidelines.

Throughout the Meeting: Members can always be reminded of the broader, deeper or more personal implications—at any stage.

The Job Is Launched

The following illustration shows how a task is given the quality of a theme, how it is formulated and then launched:

Bill Edson, the chief engineer at Copperhead Mines, noticed that inter-office memos, unit proposals and specifications were all suffering from the same malady of fuzzy, unclear writing. Staff engineers took too much time on the phone trying to clear up the muddy material that was being circulated.

Edson was no despot and didn't want to call in an outsider to "correct" the papers, school-teacher style. Realistically, he knew he'd get blank stares and snickers if he brought in a writing consultant.

Edson took a sensitive approach. He offered to help the men and women engineers put together the knowledge and skill which, as a group, they already evidenced.

Edson had an informal, pre-meeting lunch with several who were directly involved.

"I hear some of you with advanced degrees are having difficulty understanding your own memos," he began.

The response? Some joked, others were serious, but there was genuine concern for wasted time. Edson made a suggestion: "Why don't you team up and teach each other what you know about form and style in writing?"

The plan of the meeting was worked out later that afternoon by a few from the lunch meeting. They expressed the problem as a theme: "Technical Writing for Copperhead Mines: What Can We Teach Each Other? What Can We Learn from Each Other?"

At the full meeting, Edson invited the engineers to develop the task in their own way. And they did. Abbott prided himself on knowing how to give clear directions. He majored in education before switching to engineering. Katzen recalled, "When I was in school I learned best at those informal review sessions my dormmates and I would hold at all hours." Jenks, who had taken a technical writing course, summarized some of the useful things he still remembered.

The mood was warm and receptive. In the next three meetings, writing samples were exchanged. Improvement in the memos was rapid.

Telling How It's Done

It's up to you when you're the leader to keep members informed about the nuts and bolts of a meeting for two reasons. First, it gives the members a feeling of being more in control over what they are doing. Second, it takes some of the burden off your shoulders when alert members pitch in to make the process work better. Let's take "summarizing" as an example of a process the leader should establish:

A sharp disagreement arose between two points of view. There was a seesawing which threatened to dominate the rest of the meeting. The leader said to himself: "I have a hunch that if I were to summarize now, the answer would become obvious." He turned to the debaters who, by this time, were looking frayed: "Harrison and Hecht, you've made the point that there are several good small truckers who could pick up our bicycle frames. But we have to give them a day's notice. Smiley and Navelson, you claim that for a long time we've used the bigger, costlier trucker, who gives us immediate pick-ups. I thought that by summarizing, the decision will become easier." A fifth member, not part of the debate until now, jumped in with a thought: "Since we haven't had rush orders for a long time, is it really necessary to continue with the expensive trucker?" This proved to be the "obvious solution"—but not so obvious before the summary was given.

Summarizing not only spurred an effective solution from the leader's point of view, it also gave the members a tool they could use themselves to make progress if such a "seesaw situation" arose again.

When there is something wrong with the pace of a meeting, you tend to slow down, hold back and postpone decisions—like a scene in slow motion. A "frontal attack" on this decelerating condition should be deployed immediately. A leader should propose and explain the value of a time limit. A comment like this can serve to quicken the pace: "We have 30 minutes to go. Let's come up with something by then."

Or if the pace is strained and intense, find a way of loosening up the "tight collars." Tell your team: "I notice some of you have been straining to come up with perfect answers. What we can't do now, we'll do next time. Now, how about taking a few deep, quiet breaths and relaxing. We'll get more accomplished if we relieve the pressure build-up."

Leaders need not keep their methods to themselves, as in a game of poker. The more you can show that there's nothing up your sleeves but your own arms working for the goals of the meeting, the more others will join in. And members usually react to this kind of partnership with renewed efforts to make the meeting run well.

The Leader Is Neutral

Members feel more confident when they know that even if there is a "pecking order" within the organization, it'll be suspended, whenever possible, at a meeting. In the kind of meeting where everyone represents one link in a chain, those who are treated as less important will perform just as expected—as weak or missing links!

Neutrality in a leader doesn't mean blandness. You can be impartial but lively, fair but imaginative. Neutrality doesn't mean relinquishing the reins. And it doesn't mean giving "equal time" to a less knowledgeable member. Without suppressing contributions, a leader encourages those which lend quality to the process.

Being unbiased doesn't mean fading into the woodwork. A centered leader leads by safeguarding the process. But he does not occupy a raised "chair" from which he steps down every time he makes a contribution.

Dealing with Distractions

Our conscious lives are normally taken up with cycles of concentration, distraction and then a return to the original thought or action with increased energy. The same holds true at meetings where there is a continuous flow of energy in the form of concentration and distractions.

Improving efficiency requires recognizing—and exposing—these disturbances so that they can be dissipated or actually used to enhance the work. This draws members back to the task and team. When a leader understands how to deal with distractions, he or she provides a valuable form of support to the members.

Reminding members to "stay on the topic" is one of the well-known exhortations of leaders. Yet there is always a possibility that there may be a subtle or original connection between a distraction and the main topic. When a member seems to be straying, a better comment is, "Would you relate what you are saying to our task?"

Where you are quite sure that a member is going off-center, you can redirect quickly with: "Let's get back on topic now."

At a meeting of design engineers discussing a new product, Steve went off the track when he griped about getting mixed signals from two members of the consumer research division. The leader realized that Steve had become distracted from dealing with the design of the new toaster. Had this distraction been allowed to continue, it would have developed into a wasteful discussion.

Looking at Steve, the leader pointed to the theme on the board which said: "Taking the Bugs Out of the New Toaster's Automatic Timing." For a moment, Steve was taken aback by this silent gesture. Then he realized he'd lost sight of the original task and that he'd been barking up the wrong tree. He shifted quickly to the main "tree": "I think I know how to solve the problem of the automatic timing; it's set too high," and the meeting progressed.

There is also the case of Richard Harrow, usually a rather patient sort of leader, who became increasingly irritated with Phil at a planning meeting for a sales conference. A reliable contributor, generally easy to work with, Phil had been drifting off base for the first half-hour of the meeting. Richard held fire, realizing that, far from misconstruing the planning theme of the meeting, Phil was, in fact, suffering from a major distraction. To stem the flow of wasted energy, Richard asked the team to take a moment and give some brief reactions about how the meeting was going.

Phil complained, "So many members of this meeting have arrived late that I've been waiting until we're all caught up before we push ahead."

A quick summary was given to the late members, Phil proceeded in his usual goal-directed way, and Richard breathed a sigh of relief.

Had Phil been more aware of the cause of his distraction—in this case, the halted momentum due to late arrivals—he could have shared his difficulty sooner. But often, a distraction can be picked up more easily by another alert member. Just as we don't always realize when we are daydreaming, we cannot easily pick up the signals of distraction in our bodies, thoughts or feelings.

How the Ground Rules Promote the Meeting

♦ **The team must have a task formulated for the meeting.**

The task should be clear-cut, with a definable, attainable goal as the objective. Your first step? Allowing yourself to become aware of the thoughts and ideas the task immediately sets off in you, as soon as the task is presented.

♦ **There is always a team leader.**

The team leader serves as a guardian of the task or theme, and recognizes and encourages the special and unique ways that members keep the task in focus.

♦ **During each meeting, speak only for yourself.**

Representing yourself directly, rather than talking for others or in generalities, strengthens the legitimate sense of being an important asset.

♦ **Everyone must try to give—and get—from each meeting exactly what he or she wants to give and get.**

Giving means providing others freely with all the different ways you have of relating to the task. *Getting* means accepting other contributions to the theme and building on those in turn.

♦ **Nothing anyone wants to say or do is ruled out until it is heard.**

The best way to keep yourself—and others—centered on the task is by letting the distractions come through. Only by airing these normal disturbances can you become centered again. Sometimes, an off-center remark can turn out to have valuable connections to the task!

♦ **Everyone is responsible for his/her own participation.**

At most meetings, people tend to view the leader as *the* responsible person. At a *centered* meeting you're sanctioned to be your own chairperson. This frees you to deal with the task in unusual and imaginative ways because you'll be getting backup support and acceptance instead of competition and resentment.

♦ **Every meeting must end with a clear statement of what was accomplished and what remains to be done.**

Look back and evaluate your efforts at the meeting. Have you used the ground rules successfully, as tools for discovering and developing your potential for greater productivity?

These ground rules preserve the health and vitality of the meeting. When they're practiced regularly, you can answer "yes" to these frequent concerns:

- Is this meeting really necessary?
- Is *my* presence needed and wanted?
- Can I get others to understand what I want to say?
- Will the leader respect *people*, and not just the task?
- Will I be able to perform well?
- Are members' objectives for the task to be considered?
- Will there be an effort at consensus about where we are going and what we are doing?

MEMO

SUBJECT: How the leader develops the task in new ways and how he/she coaches the members once the early emotional issues are relieved.

1. The leader can <u>center</u> a task in a way that will stimulate the thoughts and associations of members beyond routine, or surface, reactions. This ensures not only precise but imaginative solutions.

2. The leader takes further hold by demonstrating to members the "nuts and bolts"—the dynamics—of the meeting.

3. Aiming at unbiased and impartial positions, the leader also should be lively and real. The leader directs his or her actions toward encouraging, stimulating, clarifying and resolving.

4. The inevitable distractions that arise are treated as natural occurrences which can actually be geared to promote the work of the meeting.

5. A review of the ground rules of a <u>centered</u> meeting shows how useful they can be at every stage, as a way of expanding the ability of every participant.

7:
The Four Elements of a Meeting

When you have an informal, unstructured conversation with someone, each of you is concerned with self-expression or what the other is saying. The process may be described as a shifting task or theme, with member elements predominating. The Team, Work and Organization parts have little or no place. But at a meeting, *all* of the components are represented. And at a *centered* meeting, these elements are put to work in ways which will now be described.

The Member Component

Being an effective member is as difficult as being a leader. A meeting throws you back on your own resources. There's a lot going on at the surface which needs your attention and awareness and action. In addition, you must bring in all you've collected from past experiences, impressions and associations.

Promise yourself that you'll exercise your ability to think, feel, sense and act. This exposure is a risk worth taking. You'll "come across" successfully if you avoid imagining or picturing yourself as less than you are. A highly self-critical picture makes you perform less effectively.

Strive to be *sincere* and *appropriate* at meetings. Sincere is whatever runs through your mind that is true to your thoughts and feelings. Appropriate is whatever fits the situation, the time and the relationship. At meetings, appropriateness is used to advance the task.

The challenge is to refrain from using the meeting as a stepping-stone to a higher rung on the organizational ladder. Rather, use a meeting as an end in itself: to be a productive member of the organization.

Caring about both procedure and content, join in the designing of the session as well as in building up ideas and facts.

I—Energy flows from living, working, growing and striving.

The Team Component

* Provide a *safe* structure in which members of different abilities and approaches can join forces.
* Relieve members of the fear of a disorganized mob or an unreasonable gang—by requiring a cooperative code of conduct.
* Offer a change of pace and relief from isolation or boredom.
* Give members a chance to be recognized and rewarded for practicing respect, cooperation and solidarity toward others.
* Offer members a way to their goals as one of a team without having to give up individuality.

II—Group energy flows from the atmosphere of the supporting—yet challenging—team.

The Work-Goal Factor

* The work-goal is what brings the meeting to life.
* The work-goal becomes the common denominator; the shared language and the joint purpose which binds members.
* The work-goal is the "finish line," the incentive—toward which members are drawn as a group.

III—Work energy comes from the central, compelling purpose and urgency of the task itself.

The Organization Factor

* An organization should provide confidence, optimism and reward.
* An organization provides an identification with power and stature.
* An organization offers challenges to grow, to advance.

IV—Organization energy flows from its rewards and protection—and sometimes from its punishments.

Working with the System

There are four elements or resources which surround—and become part of—the task.

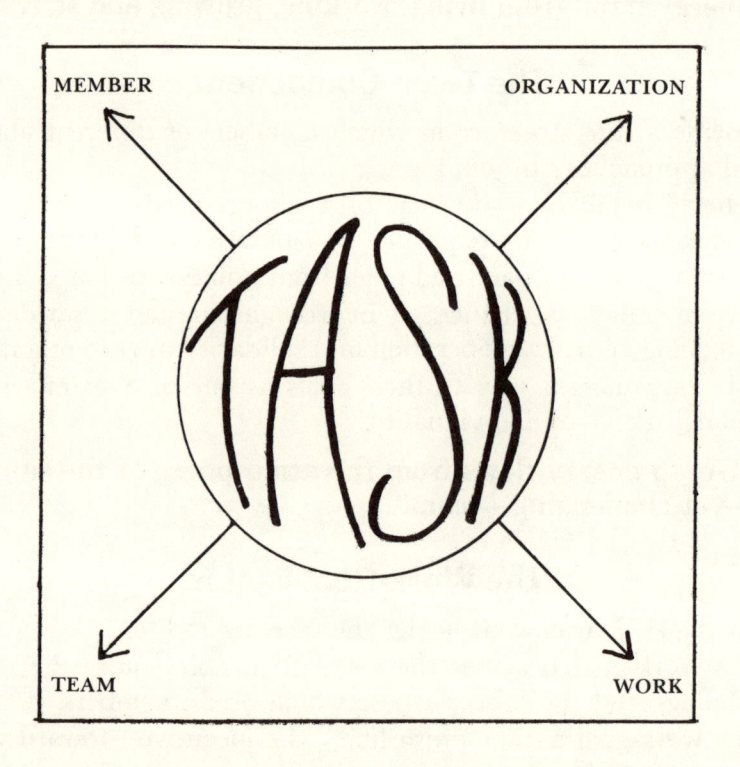

```
MEMBER                    ORGANIZATION
        ↖           ↗
             TASK
        ↙           ↘
TEAM                      WORK
```

Energy is generated at a meeting when members and leaders tap each of these four parts (Member, Team, Work and Organization) in developing and solving the task. Illustrations of how this works are often found in those exciting and unforgettable events which take place outside the walls of the office, organization or institution. These include surprise birthday parties, graduation, house purchases—and even responses to personal and national emergencies.

THE FOUR ELEMENTS

What can you learn from these occasions where so much excitement, drive and achievement are generated? Immediately, you can identify the compelling central theme or purpose. (The task of a surprise party is to bring together all the party elements—food, drinks, decorations, the birthday cake and the people—*before* the arrival of the guest of honor). Secondly, you can observe how all the resources—person, group, work and organization—are brought to bear on the central task. Real life situations are not so very different from meetings. Thus, you can observe those real life events and apply the techniques you used to your meetings.

MEMO

SUBJECT: Understanding the main structures of a meeting enables us to tap their energy.

1. Every <u>centered</u> meeting is made up of four parts which serve as sources of energy—moving the task on toward the finish line:

MEMBER power is provided by your posture (or "body language"), voice, emotional output and content of speech.

TEAM power is provided when you agree to go to a common goal together, while maintaining the life of the meeting.

WORK power is provided by your interest, urgency and satisfaction in the dealing with problems and solutions.

ORGANIZATION power comes from the base of operations it provides so there is continuity from one meeting to the next. And the organization is the source of the rewards and punishments which determine the outcome of a meeting.

2. The four elements are pictured with the task at center. This illustrates the way a meeting can be used as a coordinated system.

8:
Setting the Focus

Now you have a map showing the four main features of the meeting. As a leader you can guide members in a wide range of response choices, using Person, Team, Work and Organization elements to amplify their approach to the task. Ask your members to view the task, not alone, but in concert with any of these four elements.

Foreground and Background

Smith arrives at meetings full of ideas and enthusiasm, ready to tackle the job—yet he's ignored by everyone! What could he be doing wrong? No focus.

Smith's narrow concentration on the task—and only the task—blinds him to surrounding parts of the meeting. He neglects the background factors, which include himself, the others, the way the work is being done and the needs and presence of the organization. Naturally, his comments go unheeded. The other members get the impression that Smith is not plugged in to any of the main currents of the meeting. And while talking, he seems to be staring at his section chief. He speaks too cautiously—"too mechanically," as a friend later described it. His productivity is curtailed because he's aware of the task in foreground . . . and nothing else.

Marshall, the leader, might have helped Smith expand on his perception of the meeting and task, with a comment like: "Smith, your suggestion happens to be along the lines of what management was talking about. But can you tie in your suggestion more closely to the special slant you seem to have about company policy?" In this way, Smith's initially narrow focus can be extended. Then he can be more aware of how to work on the task in the context of the Organization.

In W. T. Galwey's *Inner Game of Tennis*, the player is told: Keep your eyes on the ball (foreground) and don't let other (background) factors crowd in. However, such elements as body movement, the opponent and spectators should be kept on the edge of awareness, not entirely shut out of your mind or vision. Well, this "athletic" advice is useful for other ordinary day-to-day patterns and structures. For instance, if your foreground task is cleaning your desk, the background might be the hum of visitors as they wait to be admitted to your office. Your awareness of this background actually makes it possible to do the desk-clearing better! Without admitting this perception of visitors into your awareness, the desk-clearing wouldn't be performed as efficiently or as completely. Believe it or not, whenever there is *total* and *exclusive* focus on something in the foreground, the result seems to be an automatic loss of interest for this object or task.

Task in Foreground

At a meeting it's important to keep the task in the foreground while maintaining one of the four elements (Member, Team, Work-Goal and Organization) in the background. You can keep an eye on the task (or "picture"), while simultaneously directing awareness to various other aspects (or "frames") of the meeting. This enriched view frees you to work with the task in a livelier way. Your will, associations, personal feelings and social stimulation all work together in service of the task.

These are the possible combinations with the task in foreground:

I. Foreground: Task . . . . Background: Personal emphasis
  II. Foreground: Task . . . . Background: Team effort emphasis
 III. Foreground: Task . . . . Background: Work procedures and goals emphasis
  IV. Foreground: Task . . . . Background: Needs of the organization emphasis

Let's see how these combinations work in actual practice at different meetings where you're a member and the task in foreground lends itself to four different "frames." In each case, you'll view the task against a different sort of background.

1. Task in foreground with your personality ("I") in background.

You underline your own personal investment and enthusiasm in the task. For instance, you say, "I would be very unhappy if this kind of product distribution contines. I have some sggestions to improve the flow."

2. Task in foreground with teamwork process (we) in background.

You're swept along—willingly—in a spontaneous team effort. For instance, everyone becomes eager to compare notes about approaches to advertising a product with slipping sales. You vote to try four of the many measures suggested to improve sales.

3. Task in foreground with work aspect (it) in background.

For instance, Jackson, who previously taught at a junior college, proposes an entirely new approach for training the next group of office machine repair people. Everyone on the training team knew the "ins and outs" of the old method. Now, thanks to Jackson, they feel refreshed and renewed about working as a team on this project.

4. Task in foreground with organization (them) in background.

For instance, Gatling agreed with the organization's drive to correct a distorted image of the company, which employees were picking up and reflecting. With his attitude of loyal commitment, Gatling can deal with the task of correcting the company's image with force and imagination.

SETTING THE FOCUS

THE FOUR COMBINATIONS WITH TASK IN <u>FOREGROUND</u>

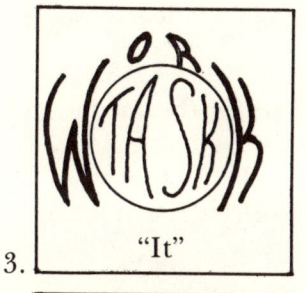

1. MEMBER / TASK — "I"

2. TEAM / TASK — "We"

3. WORK / TASK — "It"

4. ORGANIZATION / TASK — "Them"

Task in Background

In the course of any meeting, events change rapidly, producing many other pattern combinations than the ones just outlined. The task, itself, can recede into the background. And in the foreground appears the *I*, *We*, *It* or *Organization* element. This is now illustrated by a meeting devoted to "stress management."

5. Personality (I) in the foreground with task in background.

For instance, H. W. Williams stands up and offers to describe a typical day in her office, highlighting those times when stress is at its greatest and when at its least.

6. Teamwork process (we) in the foreground and task in background.

For instance, K. Rosen applauds the reduction of tension at her meeting right after several members offer to help each other.

7. Work aspect (it) in foreground and task in background.

For instance, Y. Bell gives an account of a meditation workshop he attended. He is asked how it could be applied at work.

8. Organizational aspect in foreground and task in background.

For instance, Z. Parson, the leader, reads from a report she brought from the director of her agency. It stresses the director's deep concern for the medical records of his staff. Recently, employees had suffered a rise in stress-related ailments.

THE FOUR COMBINATIONS WITH TASK IN <u>BACKGROUND</u>

5. **AS MEMBER** — "I"

6. **AS TEAM** — "We"

7. **AS WORK** — "It"

8. **AS ORGANIZATION** — "Them"

MEMO

SUBJECT: Focus on the task also must include other surrounding elements.

1. Another use of <u>centering</u> promotes Person, Work, Team and Organization elements in combination with the task. The task is kept in focus while simultaneously your attention is paid to other aspects of the meeting.

2. These may include personal reactions, support of team effort, building on procedure and content and concern for the needs of the organization.

3. The task may be seen in foreground or background while being combined with any of the four elements just as a picture and frame. Then, the task is imbued with new qualities and it may then be solved with increased energy, excitement and interest.

9:
Every Element Gets a Chance

Balancing is another essential procedure for sustaining the flow of any meeting. Its purpose is to prevent pushing too hard in one direction at the expense of other gains. At a *centered* meeting, you can deal with the four elements in a *balanced* way. Neglect and overemphasis are avoided. When the major forces are in balance:

The Member, with the needed space and recognition...

The Team, with cohesion and unity...

The Work, with its correct procedures and accurate knowledge...

The Organization, with its loyal stand behind the members and the commitment of its members...

...then all can work at maximum productivity and precision.

Identifying Neglect and Exaggeration

A meeting can become unbalanced when leader and members seek attention and glory. If there is too much "I" operating (exaggeration), the meeting breaks down into a series of solo acts by "performing members." "*I* think..." says one member. "Well, I think..." says another. "I like my idea better," says the leader. "I'm sorry, but I think I'm the only one who grasps the magnitude of this problem," another interjects, and so on.

At the opposite end is the situation in which there's not too much "I," but too little. Neglect of the "I" is seen when members react by sitting on the sidelines, holding back out of fear and caution. Think back to meetings you've attended. Remember one in which a member was manipulated or insulted or humiliated by a bully—and nothing was done to correct the inequity? Well, that was a clear case of neglect of the "I."

The team becomes unbalanced when cliques and subgroups split the meeting into warring gangs. Unlike other segments of your job, where individualistic striving and ambitious competing are rewarded, a meeting requires *swimming*—or *sinking*—together. The team needs to work as a whole, balancing weaker and stronger members.

On the other hand, sometimes the intense brotherhood that can develop within a team can smother other important movements in a meeting. For instance, group leader Erwin Steele asked his members to come up with individual reports on the new products convention they attended. Instead, the team handed in one report, "homogenizing" their individual and unique views into one "milky" opinion.

The work element becomes unbalanced when members are so taken up with the work itself, that they act like drones in a beehive. An illustration of this may be seen at a meeting of the Klean Kitchen Cabinet Division. Biggs, a division head, stated the problem: "Our company was losing out to a competitor who was winning a large share of the market by reducing its price—and sacrificing profit—on the most popular, ready-made kitchen cabinet in the industry. I was told by the president, 'You have the personnel to handle the problem; see what you can do.' This sounded like an ultimatum, causing me more than one restless night."

At the beginning of the meeting, Biggs had the good sense to suggest working on a plan to compete with the price-cutting competitor. He wanted to add some attractive cabinet locks—while holding to the same price.

Unfortunately, Biggs had a tendency to tighten up under stress. He was very tense about the possibility that the success of the plan —increased efficiency—could not be accomplished with the people he'd invited to the meeting. They consisted of two skilled supervisors of production, the sales manager and several salespeople, and a representative from quality control. It wasn't going to be easy to get them coordinated.

Early in the meeting, Biggs got bogged down in a long discussion about the specifications of the new hardware. Then, suddenly realizing that salespeople were present, he turned to the question of how best to present the new cabinet to buyers. Swept along by this frantic attention to the work element, the quality control representative listed ways the new product could be inspected.

By this time, Biggs sensed that something had gone stale. There was a lot of buzzing and darting, but little progress. Everyone remained locked inside the boundaries of their particular jobs and a free exchange of ideas never got off the ground. With a sinking feeling, he realized that he was getting nowhere. The meeting ended in confusion and dissatisfaction.

The organization element also becomes unbalanced when it places undue influence and emphasis on itself. If the meeting is to fulfill its purpose, it cannot become simply an echo of what the management wants to hear. The setting becomes totally organization-oriented, and therefore unbalanced. This causes negative tremors. Insensitive personnel policies force members to fight back through apathy or uncontrollable anger. These reactions may be traced back to unresolved complaints about the organization.

How Balancing Works

A good balance of all features results in a meeting which works like a healthy organism. Each "organ" functions independently—and yet interdependently. In this way, you can devote your efforts to tending the task while performing well and helping others at the same time.

Study the following meeting of experienced staff members at a department store chain. It illustrates the concept of balancing. The members, as well as the leader, corrected a problem of overloading and restored balance.

Ralph, an assertive, outgoing sales manager holds center stage for 20 minutes, enthusiastically describing how he used a new sales technique he developed. His stories were so good that no one stopped him, even though he was wasting time. When finally he finished, other members jumped in with their own monologues about selling methods. (Too much "*I*.")

Joan thought silently that these testimonials were interesting and entertaining—but one-sided. They neglected the objective of the meeting—to examine the new distribution procedure. She wondered how to stop this derailing of the meeting. Joan decided to say to Ralph in a voice everyone could hear: "I tried that method but it doesn't work for me. Maybe it's because I have less secretarial help."

Ralph said, "Joan, I think that I forgot to take into account other people's working conditions. I can see my method wouldn't work without secretarial support."

There followed an exchange about their working styles and work priorities related to the new distribution method. This opened the meeting to other refreshing comparisons and renewed enthusiasm. (Too much *I* balanced by *We*.)

James, known for his meticulous working habits, sensed an imbalance and joined in. He said, "I don't want to sound like a wet rag but I'm not clear about something regarding this meeting. Am I supposed to be dealing with the new distribution plan as it works in different areas of the city, or is the task to evaluate the mechanics of the procedure itself? The meeting announcement didn't make this clear."

Actually, both parts of the question were encompassed by the task as it had been announced by the leader at the start of the meeting. But James saw the beginning of an overemphasis on reactions between members. His contribution was to bring in a more factual and logical approach to the task. (Too much *We* balanced by *It*.)

There followed much talk about the task itself. Jenny went into detail about the limits of the goal of the meeting. Others followed with comments about "nailing it down" and "putting it together." The *It* factor began to dominate—to the neglect of individual creativity or team effort. Productive activity was drying up.

Terry, vice-president of sales and leader of the meeting, made a balancing move by saying: "I seem to have rushed the deadline for evaluating our distribution plan. The company really is interested in having your careful thinking on this. I'd like to suggest that you've been asked to bite off too big a piece. Let's just explore it today and wrap it up next meeting." (Too much *It* balanced by a reminder of the context or the *Organization*.)

Balancing can be a simple and powerful action by members and leader, since it steadies the whole "ship" of the meeting. Sometimes it requires taking a step back for a moment and looking at the movement of the meeting. Are the four "sails" (*I*, *We*, *It*,

Organization) producing a steady forward movement? Or is one sail catching more breeze and pushing the ship off course? A slight shift of emphasis, as just illustrated, permits the ship to make full speed to its destination.

THE BALANCING ACT OF A CENTERED MEETING

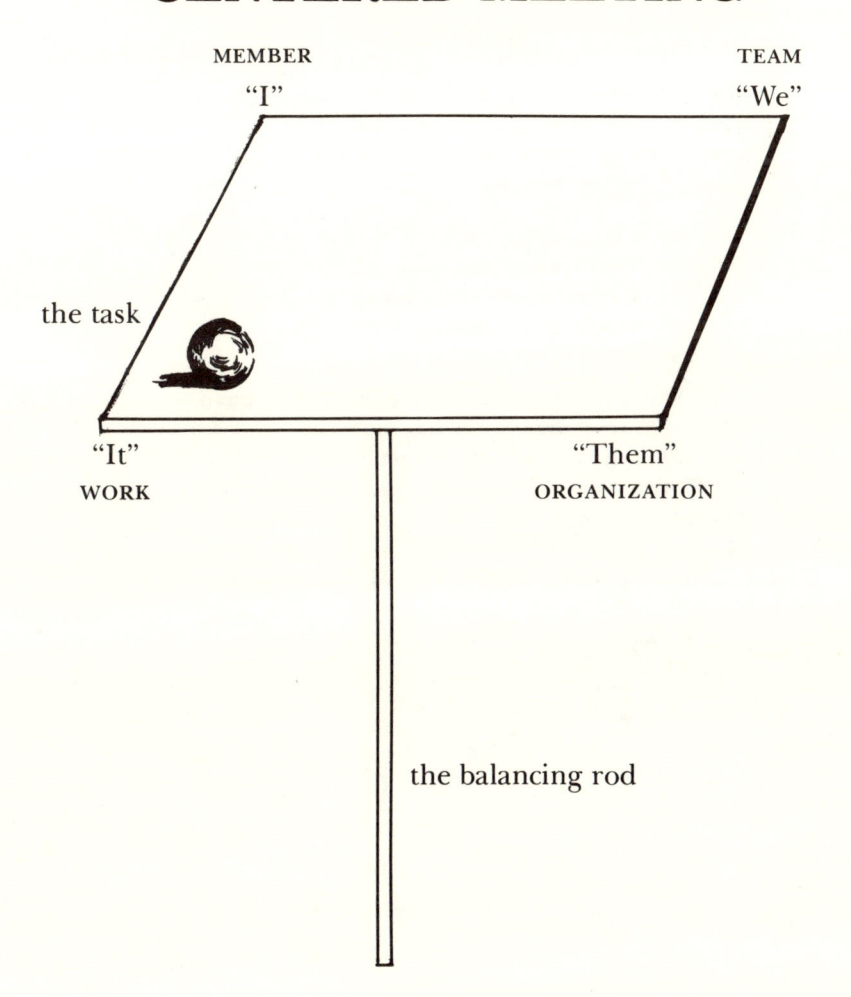

```
         MEMBER              TEAM
          "I"                 "We"

the task

         "It"               "Them"
         WORK             ORGANIZATION


              the balancing rod
```

Balancing takes place as on the surface of a smooth table (Meeting) with a steel ball (Task) rolling from one corner to another (The Four Elements). The task is kept in motion by the tilting action of the member holding the rod. As the ball hits each corner, a point is scored and it moves on to the next corner with renewed energy and impetus.

MEMO

SUBJECT: By balancing the four operating elements of a meeting, you can make sure that each of them contributes its full and proportionate share.

1. At a <u>centered</u> meeting you enjoy the advantage of using all four sails—or operating elements—of a meeting. In guarding against their overemphasis or underemphasis, you use balancing.

2. Participants can sense when too much time has been spent in one kind of movement. In fact, this kind of overemphasis is boring. Shift the "weight" in another directon and restore the meeting to a level course—on all its four sails.

10:
Your Inner Zone

If you're to work, share, compete and communicate effectively at meetings you'll need to get in contact with your inner zone. It is here that your "natural" feelings reside—feelings of weakness, strength, anger and love. In his book, *Toward a Psychology of Being*, A. Maslow wrote about the directness, clarity and power you can wield if you express your feelings from your inner core, without filtering them. When you filter, or adopt a façade, you're seen as distant, detached and "half-real." By speaking from your inner zone, your feelings fit appropriately into what you're saying and doing. A façade makes you overly concerned with the reactions of others. For instance, if while you're making an important suggestion you get angry at a meeting member for not paying attention, you might express that feeling directly by saying, "Ed, I'm proposing a system that directly affects your department. I'd appreciate your attention so I won't have to repeat it later."

If you masked this feeling, you'd wind up sounding like this: "It's your fault I never get my proposals approved. You never listen—so how can you know if you like them?" (Notice the tone of blame and attack?) As a result of maintaining this "wall of distance," your energy is wasted and productivity is crippled.

In the following diagram, first see how your natural feelings can be sustained from inner core to outer expression. At the façade, or surface, important and useful feelings are transformed (through fear) into artificial and pallid expressions.

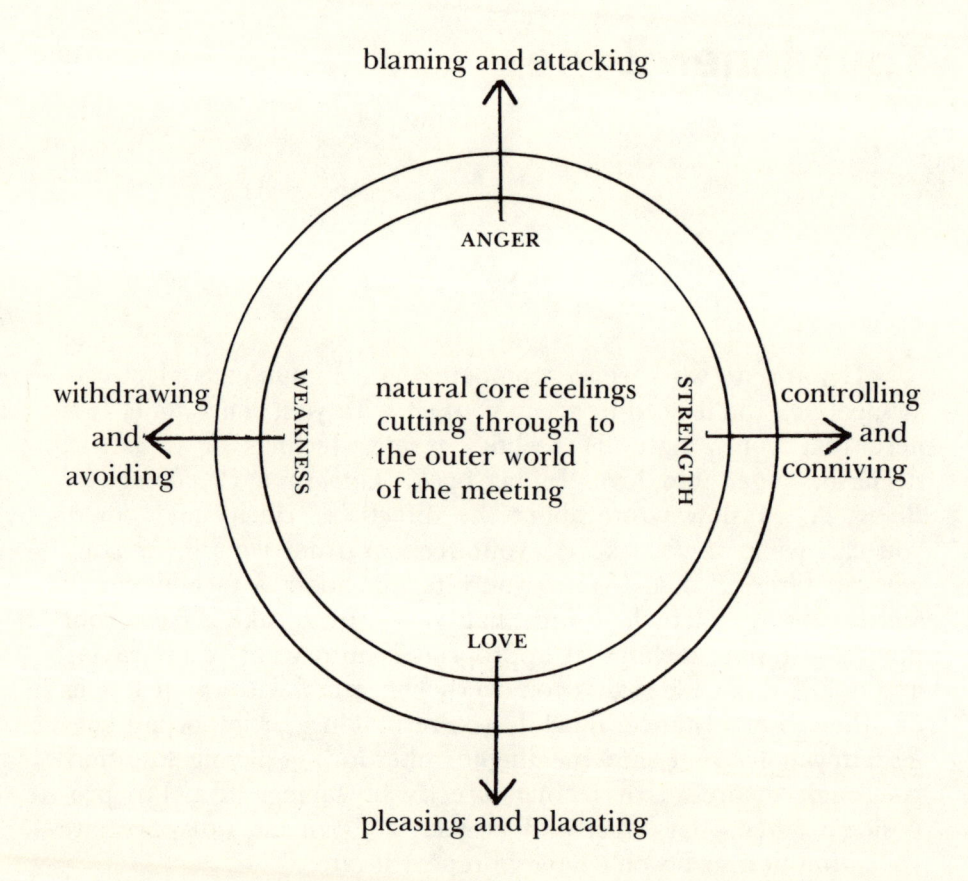

```
                    ↑ blaming and attacking
                    |
                 ANGER
      ┌──────────────────────────┐
      │                          │
withdrawing  W   natural core feelings   S   controlling
   and    ← E   cutting through to   → T →  and
avoiding     A   the outer world      R    conniving
             K   of the meeting       E
             N                        N
             E                        G
             S                        T
             S                        H
      │                          │
      └──────────────────────────┘
                 LOVE
                    |
                    ↓
              pleasing and placating
```

To illustrate: If at a meeting you get *angry* because your opinions aren't requested and you think you're being overlooked, apply this feeling directly. Call attention to the points you wish to make with strength and insistence. If you masked these feelings, you'd have to convert your *anger* into *blaming and attacking*.

The other core feelings also are subject to being disguised. Feelings of *love and admiration* often are seen as "risky" emotions. So, they're reduced to *pleasing and placating. Strength* invites retaliation, so it's converted into *controlling and conniving*. Finally, *weakness* is felt as being only a step away from nonexistence, so it is reprocessed into *withdrawing and avoiding*.

When R. F. Bales, in his book *Interaction Process Analysis: A Method for the Study of Small Groups*, classified all the basic ways in which a member's effectiveness can be crippled at meetings, he showed how the categories correspond to the façades erected against the inner zone of expression.

* When you're so preoccupied with safeguarding your own security and hiding your feelings, you can't pay attention to the task.
* When you're not feeling accepted, you become unfriendly.
* When you're unsure of how to use your strength, or feel your position is weak, you may come on either overcontrolling or excessively withdrawing.

How much—and how well—you operate from the core is not always within your immediate control. Sometimes, extremely threatening situations require defenses. You need a façade when you must "save face" or appear braver than you feel in order to maintain equilibrium and a minimal sense of well-being. If you're in touch with your inner core, you'll know when you're about to adopt a façade. Then you can ask yourself: "Is this façade really necessary and helpful? Or should I tell them straight-out?"

Use this guide at meetings to help you tap your inner zone:

1. Permit yourself to concentrate fully on your inner self to get in touch with the effect others are having on you.
2. Seek out opportunities to risk, grow and learn. It is fear that makes you play it safe.
3. Work hard at developing your potential into several strong points. Then you won't have to settle for being second best.
4. Center on the task by making it a part of you.

MEMO

SUBJECT: The importance of bringing more of yourself into every meeting.

1. By expressing yourself directly, clearly and in depth, your message emerges as real and convincing. Avoid screening and filtering what you intend to say and you'll avoid indirect, confusing signals.

2. Self-actualizing people are highly productive because they can concentrate on the task without getting sidetracked in covering up. They can be recognized in these general ways:

* They employ fully their own talent and ability.
* They care as much for problems near and far around themselves as they do for themselves.
* They give more than they take.
* They have acceptance of and respect for themselves while achieving self-control and self-discipline.
* They can be an integrated part of a meeting while maintaining a non-conforming aspect—expressed not angrily but as related to their own values.
* They enjoy to their fullest, feelings, sensations, perceptions and abstractions within the framework of productive activity.

11:
Your Best Foot Forward

By now you have developed deeper and more candid self-expression. You've achieved this by: observing ground rules #3, 4, 5, and 6; by operating from your inner zone; applying the principles of self-actualization and by removing your masks and defenses. Hopefully, you've seen some results already. But now you must learn the *practical subtleties* of candid self-expression so you won't get hurt in the process. You are about to learn how to *moderate* (not hide) your authentic, core responses. Later in this chapter, you'll find additional ways of putting your best foot forward by establishing credibility, reconciling opposite feelings and sending and receiving accurate body signals.

Moderate Responses

Moderate—rather than extreme—responses, which are based on healthy core feelings, are more palatable at meetings. The following are examples of moderate responses by confident team members. You'll notice they encourage the less self-confident to drop their wasteful defenses. The best responses reflect warmth, openness, sensitivity and appropriateness.

Warmth. Sheryl is so naturally friendly and outgoing that it's easy for her to be understanding of others. Even when a chronic latecomer arrives, Sheryl sustains her warm and tolerant manner. "Have a seat next to Roland, Kate. We're well into a discussion of how to promote our new wallpaper designs. Erik, will you continue, please?" She neither rewards nor punishes Kate for arriving late.

Openness. Russell's preferred style is what he calls "constructive confrontation." He doesn't hesitate to reveal how a certain assignment has affected the pace and quality of his work. "This project will take three weeks. I'm putting everything else aside. My mail is piling up but I think it can wait."

Sensitivity. Luckman, a rather staid gentleman, gives the impression of being very fussy about details. But surprisingly, he's a model of sensitivity, even in his role as a law enforcement officer in a governmental agency. By careful *listening, observing* and *empathizing*, he has induced several underworld figures to turn informers on a major racket that his department is prosecuting.

Appropriateness. At a meeting, Singman has the effect of a gyroscope—keeping everyone on an even keel. He has a flair for balancing himself in most situations. Saying what he means—even if it involves angry feelings—without covering up, he "clears the air" quickly and effectively. He avoids bringing in his personal problems, although when his child was seriously ill, he explained that this was the cause of his distraction. He competes in a playful, rather than war-like manner, without withdrawing from the scene when under stress. "Joe, your department got the best sales figures this quarter. I'm just putting you on notice: my team is out to beat that record next quarter!"

At times, you've got to delay or defer expression of your feelings to save a meeting from serious interference.

Team leader Nestor Kaplan's members hadn't quite recovered from the resignation of a well-liked unit chief. Kaplan found that their disappointment and fears were spilling over into the meetings —in the form of confused and disjointed discussions. Their intense feelings of loss couldn't be aired and dissolved quickly, and therefore threatened to absorb the entire time of the meeting. Kaplan said, "The meeting is in danger of falling apart. Is this what you want? The objectives of this meeting are important and should not be neglected even though someone you admired greatly has resigned. I'd like to ask you this: Can you use your strength of will to moderate your feelings and carry out your responsibilities as team members?"

Needless to say, each member around the table nodded in silent assent—and the meeting progressed from there.

You've Got To Be Believed

When you're "all there"—that is, conscious, concentrating and aware—you can deposit all your "capital" in the bank of the meeting. But also consider how you can go about raising your "credibility." How can you be seen as trustworthy?

Studies of people who attract the confidence of others show five ways of achieving this advantage:

1. Your credibility is earned by demonstrating a good grasp of the subject of a meeting.

2. Your credibility is enhanced by your belief in the power of a meeting.

3. Your credibility is raised by your willingness to drop the mask you usually wear when you're intent on selling yourself. In this case, less selling makes a better sale.

4. Your credibility is strengthened if you are more active and interactive—so that others feel you're in contact with them.

5. Your credibility is insured when you display an alertness and sensitivity to what is going on *now* as opposed to dwelling on the past or future events.

Your reputation as a person to be believed is more than just a self-serving badge of honor and recognition. Not only do you win sincere respect for yourself but you get the job of the meeting done by raising the trust level of others on the team.

Opposite Ends Work Together

There is another way to make good use of feelings and it is what F. S. Perls, in his book *Gestalt Therapy Verbatim*, calls "reconciling opposites." There are many sets of opposite feelings and conflicts you experience daily:

- "Should I write a letter next week or make a call now?"
- "Should I anticipate every wish of the boss or should I work independently of his opinions?"
- "Should I act tough or sensitive?"

When you reconcile opposites, you make them serve your purpose in a balanced way that is most natural for you. First you must isolate the extremes. In the first conflict above, no distinction is made between the merits of the telephone call and writing the letter. The differences tend to blur even though the two are far apart. On one hand is the advantage of the immediate contact of a telephone call; on the other is the avoidance "cushion" of the less direct form of contact, the letter.

Once the two sides are clarified, less energy is spent in conflict. The two sides, now better defined and "resting in their opposite corners," can accommodate themselves to each other, by moving toward the center. Now you can solve the problem in a balanced way. You might choose neither to phone nor write. Or, the solution might be an improved phone call or letter, or a combination of the two.

A meeting, with its rich play of events, sprouts many opposites. Members who reconcile and center the conflicts tend to have clear voices and make decisive actions. Consider the relevance of the following two-sided issues. Can you begin to see the opposites clearly?

One Part of Me	**The Other Part of Me**
1. I stand entirely on my own two feet.	I buckle at the knees—always leaning on someone.
2. I lead the team to victory—and nothing but victory.	I retreat to the rear—and just follow along.
3. I compete ruthlessly.	I cooperate with complete self-effacement.
4. I give out with my entire being.	I take whatever I can get greedily.
5. I trust everyone's words and actions—like a trusting child holding on to its father's hand.	I distrust to the point of total suspicion.
6. I consider the authority of the leader to be unassailable.	I consider the authority of the leader as something to be opposed automatically.
7. I pledge total loyalty to the team and organization, who made it possible for me to be here.	I reserve all my loyalty for myself. I am Number One.

8. I express dissatisfaction by *exiting*—turning attention away from the welfare of the meeting to another part of the organization.	I express dissatisfaction by *voicing* harsh criticism within the meeting.
9. I maintain complete security by not sticking out my neck—even if I don't gain any ground in the process.	I often overextend myself and take risks, even at the expense of my safety and survival.
10. I hold on to mechanical, preset roles.	I adopt manifold roles without consciously choosing them; they "just happen."
11. I am a model of such unqualified sincerity as to be almost embarrassing.	I believe in adhering to conventional proprieties of behavior at all costs—even if it means giving up my own personal style or unique ways of thinking or doing things.

After facing these two sides squarely, begin to sort them out. Then, let a more balanced compromise between the two take over.

The Body Speaks Loudly

The purpose of developing an awareness of non-verbal signals is to improve working relationships among team members. (Knowledge of body language at a meeting won't give you any "secret weapons" you can use for attacking an unsuspecting victim. This mode of aggression is best left to those intent only on winning, rather than relating productively.)

The non-verbal cues you send out may be voluntary or involuntary. The voluntary cues convey information about yourself which you want transmitted. When, for example, Carlos Santilla comes to a meeting, he establishes successfully by his sure, suave manner and his sophisticated style of dress that he: takes pride in his physical prowess; enjoys challenging others; is somewhat of a rebel; values his highly developed skill as a land surveyor, and comes from a fine family of Spanish origin.

Your body also speaks involuntarily—from the moment you enter the meeting room and sit down. Take your choice of seat, for example. Do you seek a location of focus (out of a feeling of dominance), or do you choose a seat which places you with the crowd? Do you sit down close to others in a cozy or collusive way or do you look for an isolated or independent location?

Not every message can—or needs to—be decoded. You may enter the meeting with strong religious or aesthetic feelings or you may be happy about your good health, but unless you express them directly, others need have no connection with these highly personal states. What you're interested in are the *usable* messages locked in the body:

1. A rigid body goes with an unbending rigidity of ideas.
2. A chin up is part of a courageous, optimistic view.
3. A thrust-out jaw goes with determination.
4. A slumped body reflects a weak and defeated personality.
5. Raised shoulders with withdrawn neck suggest fear.
6. Eyes carry anger, fear, softness, directness or evasiveness.
7. Lines on the forehead show surprise, astonishment or uncertainty.

These messages and many more are sensed even by young children and animals. When understood, they can help the receiver respond with greater sensitivity and comprehension. There are further instances of how these multi-channel messages are used profitably.

From the sender. Get in touch with your own body signals. See if you can find any mixed messages you might be sending. For instance, is your voice controlled while your heart beats rapidly? Or are you smiling while your knees are locked in fear? Your head is turned toward someone, but are your toes pulling in the opposite direction?

Mixed messages, such as these, cause strain and tension while diluting the impact of your contribution. To remove the obstacles which are tying you up in the first place, consider the following questions:

♦ Are your fears exaggerated?
♦ Are you adequately prepared?
♦ Are you too indirect and unassertive?
♦ Would you like to have more support but fear asking for it?
♦ Are you trying to play politics when you shouldn't?

Begin at the beginning. Try to imagine yourself speaking from a relaxed sitting position. Your feet are in good solid contact with the floor; backbone is straight but not rigid; breathing is deep—from the diaphragm; words come out as you breathe out; gaze is directly at your audience. Now position yourself just as you did in your mind. Starting off in a comfortable position helps you to think, speak and get ideas across directly. You may be pleasantly surprised at the results of this simple technique first of visualizing, then of actualizing your own relaxation.

Some actions or behaviors that supplement words are neither harmful nor helpful and, therefore, need not be worked on:

Smith hitches his socks or adjusts his glasses often.

Anders brushes a lock of hair from her forehead just before asking a question.

Robin clears her throat when trying to get into the discussion.

Kenneth makes a chopping motion with his right hand to establish his point more strongly.

These movements are often ingrained. When they don't distract others, they need not require further analysis or changing.

From the receiving end. Some nonverbal messages are deeply effective without your realizing it. It can be jarring if a member sitting next to you, caught up in the whirl of a meeting, happens to touch you on the arm or hand. For "no touch" people, this is hard to handle since it represents an invasion of your "body privacy." If you recognize your "touchy" feelings—but realize this is an insignificant accident—you can avoid blowing it out of proportion.

A harsh or monotonous voice also can be irritating if you're overly sensitive. As a piano-tuner, your aural sensitivities would be appropriate. But don't become obsessed with trivia at a meeting. After all, aren't your rough edges often tolerated or ignored in the interests of harmony? Be honest.

Opportunities will always exist where your sensitivity to nonverbal signals can be extremely useful. Senior partner Eric Singer is particularly good at this. He picked up the tension and annoyance surrounding the words of the speaker at a recent meeting, but reacted to the feelings *behind* the words. He said, "I know you have some negative opinions about this. I have strong feelings about it, too. Let's try comparing notes." Singer picked up the signal of restless, shuffling feet of several members and suggested, "There seems to be tension in the air. Let's talk about what's going on." This helped change the pace and redirect the energy that was being wasted at the meeting.

In another instance, let's suppose that Harold is squirming in his seat and tapping his finger while you're giving a summary of your project. Interpreting this nonverbal message can lead in any one of several directions: Have I been taking up too much time? Did I overlook what Harold said previously? Or is Harold impatient about something else quite unconnected to what I'm saying?

You'll be guided to the most accurate interpretation if you let yourself relax and feel and sense freely. The answer almost seems to come by itself—if you let it. The conclusion you'd come to in this case is: *Harold's impatience can't be due to any pushiness on my part—my manner has been firm but reasonable. Instead, probably he's unhappy about the lack of recognition he got for related work he completed last year. Even though Harold "waves his own flag," he can't call this former achievement to our attention now. As a senior member of the unit, he realizes—for good reasons—that such a competitive announcement would clip the wings of our own sense of accomplishment.*

Coming to an accurate interpretation can then free you to be generous. Think of the smile you'd put on Harold's face (not to mention the future cooperation you'd get from him) if you said, "I'd like to mention that Harold conducted a similar project last year, and although it's not widely known, he achieved great success with it."

MEMO

SUBJECT: Putting your best foot forward means giving responses which are moderate, yet based on the strong emotional signals within you.

1. Moderate responses, creating an atmosphere of cooperation and trust, should include warmth, openness, sensitivity and appropriateness.

2. Even if, by character, you are honest and sincere at a meeting, your reputation for credibility must be established through specific actions.

3. Non-verbal signals help you understand more about what's really being said. The purpose of paying attention to body language is to find better ways of relating to your "partners in productivity."

12:
Removing Communication Roadblocks

One of the first things a leader does to promote a productive discussion is to emphasize *listening*.

A good listener lets a speaker know the effect he or she is having. This response must be clear and appropriate so the speaker accepts it willingly without feeling attacked or imposed upon. Give the speaker your full attention, maintaining a critical "ear."

The effective *sending* of messages starts with this attitude of the speaker: "I belong here and I have the right to assert my ideas." This attitude should be encouraged regularly by the leader because no one ever feels completely secure about speaking out.

Words, the raw material of meetings, are the most powerful form of communication. They're the chief way in which you can influence others. Words take on different meanings, depending on who speaks—and how—and on the special associations and interpretations you make to what is said. Nevertheless, you can learn to use words better to promote clear discussions and to *hear* words better to improve your understanding of the message.

Screen messages for their directness, clarity, relevance, quality of organization and overall contribution to the meeting. If you are leader, notice when words, or responses to them, are fuzzy or misleading and try to stop this wasted effort. How? First, you can serve as a model by sending clear messages. Second, use key, penetrating questions or suggestions to encourage communication.

Preventing Blocked Ideas and Messages

The following are seven examples of obstacles preventing the flow of communication circulation and how you can remove them. They will be analyzed in this order:

1. Insufficient clues to the meaning of a word.
2. Danger of generalizing.
3. Transfer of your thoughts to someone else.
4. How self-image gets in the way of delivery.
5. Message without frame weakens the message.
6. The automatic veto cuts down communication and team work.
7. A mixed message must be recognized and corrected.

Communication Block #1: Insufficient Clues to the Meaning of a Word

Situation:

Morning lateness has spread throughout the accounting department at Rydell Advertising. A meeting is called to explore the problem.

Message:

SMITH (one of the latecomers): Getting to work at 8:30 A.M. is pretty rough.

LEADER: What do you mean? The words "pretty rough" say a lot to you but have a different meaning to others. "Pretty rough" for some is agonizing pain; for others it is only a slight itch. Smith, are you suggesting that some of us would function better if we staggered our hours?

Communication Problem:

What often appears to be an obvious statement actually has a special meaning to the person who said it. For Smith, early hours are so "rough" that the idea of staggered arrivals, once voiced by the leader, sounds like an appealing solution. Smith sets to work on writing up a proposal for staggered conditions.

Communication Block #2: Danger of Generalizing

Situation:

At Bolton's Bolt Company, small parts take too long getting out to the assembly line. Complaints are voiced.

Message:

FACTORY MANAGER: I'm disgusted! No one can find anything in the stockroom.

PRODUCTION CHIEF: Why did you go in there alone? Wasn't there anyone in the cage?

FACTORY MANAGER: Well, I stood there for a while. Someone was rummaging around in the back of the room—but he never came out.

PRODUCTION CHIEF: This always happens in our busy season.

LEADER (to Production Chief): Jack, have you been in that maze recently to look for parts? I wonder if we need another clerk to do some of the legwork.

Communication Problem:

Generalizations about who, what, where or when can be dangerously misleading. One or more instances do not represent *all* instances. The factory manager was right about *his* not finding certain things. But his generalizing could have led to the inference that *no one* could *ever* find *anything*. The leader recognized this and uncovered the real problem.

Communication Block #3: Transfer of Your Thoughts to Someone Else

Situation:

ABC Company had an agreement with Sebastian to stay on in the branch office for two more months to iron out some computer programming problems. Sebastian agreed hesitantly because family commitments required his return to his home city. At a meeting, several key members of the computer section expressed their eagerness to have him stay longer: "You're doing a good job and we want to win that new contract, so how about seeing the project through to completion?"

Message:

OFFICE MANAGER: I know what you're going through. When you think of staying on, it's like saying goodbye to your host and then returning an hour later because you missed the train.

SEBASTIAN: Well . . . I—can't exactly say that's how I feel . . .

LEADER (to Office Manager): Sebastian may not be thinking about it in that way. If you thought about it, I'm sure you'd realize some other possible reasons Sebastian may have. Sometimes we forget that others are separate and unique and that we have to listen carefully to hear the differences.

Communication Problem:

The office manager assumed too quickly that Sebastian had the same thoughts and perceptions as she. The leader's comment gave Sebastian a chance to think more clearly about what he really needed and wanted, balanced against the needs of the company. His decision was to stay on—but to go home for a week's visit first.

Communication Block #4:
Self-Image Gets in the Way

Situation:

Sales managers at Orion Knitwear are meeting with the production staff to do something about promised orders that are not delivered to buyers because of production delays.

Message:

HARRIS (from Production): I realize that what I want to say doesn't fit in exactly but I must fill in some background facts for the people here in sales.

LEADER: Don't apologize, Harris. When any one of us feels unsure, this negative image gets in the way of delivery. Communication lines break down. First, the sender is distracted from the main task or message. Then he sends out less relevant, more indirect messages concerning who he is or what he wants. Finally, the receivers treat these unimportant messages with indifference.

To keep the communication lines intact, talk straight—not up or down—to your team members. Avoid self-conscious apologies. If you redirect your energies to the goal of the meeting, it will lead to better recognition and response.

Communication Problem:

Harris, who is in production, feels his status is lower than those in distribution. At this meeting, he retreated to a silent, listening position. This weakened the influence which he deserved and wanted. Then, changing his stance, Harris tried to impress the distribution people with a display of information. Again Harris was defeated—his contribution taken all too casually by the others. His poor self-image had weakened and diverted him from the team work.

Communication Block #5:
Message Is Weakened Without a Frame

Situation:

The monthly marketing meeting of a chemical conglomerate.

Message:

FRED (Advertising Manager): All of you received copies of the marketing report I finished last month. But since then, I've gotten very little feedback about it. When some of the data in the report came up in this meeting, it seemed like it was all new to you. I must have sounded impatient because it reminded me that I hadn't gotten any reactions from you in a whole month. What I really want to say is, "How about listening to me more carefully?"

LEADER: You're right, Fred, and I'm to blame, too. You sent a copy to me and I didn't answer. I'd like to ask everyone who hasn't done so, to give Fred a response by this Friday—either face-to-face or by memo. I'll be sure to give it priority for the next meeting.

MEMBER: Fred, we got the whole message this time—the frame *and* the picture. It's not just the report. You're also saying that we don't pay enough attention.

Communication Problem:

Fred, the sender, has overcome the problem. Now he offers a better opportunity for receivers to hear the surface message as well as the sender's deeper meaning.

Communication Block #6: The Automatic Veto

Situation:

At a meeting of food service managers, Abrams asked whether

anyone had heard from the CEO about renewing personnel contracts for next year. In this example, the listener reacts to the wrong part of the message.

Message:
TINA (Manager of another unit): If you need job security, I can think of places in government service that will do this for you. I hope you take this in the right way—but in this industry, there is very little security.

LEADER: Tina, it's good to hear you saying what's on your mind, and I like working with you because of this. You have a radar screen which picks up important things. But this time, I don't think you heard the real message. Abrams wasn't emphasizing "job security" at all. If you waited for the message to sink in for an extra moment, you wouldn't have made such a quick veto.

Communication Problem:
The receiver is often an instant reactor. These trigger responses don't give the receiver a chance to think about what was said. They also encourage *prescribing solutions* rather than *describing dimensions of problems*.

Communication Block #7: Mixed Messages
Situation:
A meeting of employees and managing executives of a publishing company are trying to get a cross section of opinion on the need for a company insurance plan. After a meeting, the vice-president of personnel assigned Jack, a capable assistant to the finance officer, to follow through in gathering more data—a rather tedious job.

Message:
JACK (with a trace of a smile): I'll be glad to take care of the darned thing.

KIM (trying to be helpful): Jack, like most of us, it sounds like you realize there's never enough time to get everything done around here.

LEADER: Kim, you did pick up an important part of the message. But Jack gave a mixed message. He smiled, but he also called his task that "darned thing." He seems to be asking for help, protesting a bit—and perhaps wanting to be left alone to do the job by himself—all at once. Unless we check it out as a team, we'd just be guessing.

REMOVING COMMUNICATION ROADBLOCKS

Roadblock	Removal
1. One word can have different meanings.	Ask what the word means when it is unclear or has several meanings.
2. A generalized, sweeping statement is made with no proof.	Question it as a fact and point out exceptions.
3. A personal conclusion or interpretation is imposed on someone else's statement.	Verify what you think was meant before drawing conclusions.
4. A negative self-image gets in the way of your presentation.	Suspend negative self-evaluations while sending messages.
5. The message lacks context or frame, and is delivered in a surface way.	Give the background of the message—the feeling behind it and the timing.
6. The listener rejects or weakens the message.	First, listen carefully for an area of agreement or for a way you can limit the dimensions of the *problem*, before responding.
7. Contradictory or paradoxical parts of a single message are dovetailed.	Sort out the mixed message and respond to each component separately.

Communication Problem:

Jack's message was mixed; he was challenged, pleased and uncomfortable, all at the same time. Kim, the receiver, neglected to sort out the inconsistent message. She responded only to Jack's sense of pressure about time.

MEMO

SUBJECT: How leaders monitor the use of words to improve the exchange of ideas and information.

1. A good leader can determine whether members in a discussion are using words to work together, to compete excessively or to stand still at a roadblock.

2. Make certain that everyone's words and messages are promoting the functions of the meeting rather than choking them. The leader can help identify and remove these seven blocks:

- Sometimes a word has an approximate and hazy meaning, and listeners interpret it in their own ways.
- Generalizations, such as the use of "always," "never" or "everybody," distort reality and truth.
- Assumptions that everyone is like you and thinks the same prevent seeing that we think in separate and unique ways.
- Preoccupations about yourself can be so pervasive as to overwhelm your words.
- The speaker has an underlying message—often in the form of an attitude toward what he or she is saying—which isn't heard or even detected in the surface message.
- The listener reacts instantly—impulsively—and then prescribes solutions not based on what the speaker meant.
- In a mixed message, two contradictory statements are made at the same time, leaving the receiver confused.

13:
More Than You Think

A meeting is an invitation to stretch your psychological muscles to the utmost. These "muscles" include: 1) rational thinking, 2) sensing and feeling, 3) willing and behaving.

Rational Thinking

The level of your rational thinking is determined by such abilities as logic, abstracting, concentration, memory, creativity, reflectiveness and attention. Education, training and practice can have important effects upon your intelligence. This is why you can prepare for a meeting knowing that your level of thinking can always be improved.

To tie the best of your abilities to the goals of the meeting, you can use both *free-wheeling*, as well as the more controlled *analytic* thinking. Freer thinking allows you to "bounce off" from someone else's point without connecting with it directly. It is more imaginative and creative, and frees you to make personal associations to what has just occurred.

In this example of free-wheeling thinking, Mark Jordan of Petite Pea Farms, wanted to improve taste by shortening the time it took to get peas from the field to the freezer. Sitting opposite was Barbara Salem, from sales, who made a seemingly unrelated humorous comment: "This reminds me that, by the time certain reports get to our office, the information is already stale and there's no further point in sending back an answer." This comment actually served the purpose of emphasizing and enriching the overall theme of saving time and improving product quality.

The level and flow of discussion depend also on *analytic* thinking, which is a way of understanding the component parts of a situation and how they fit together. Tina Sheba, also present at the above meeting, used this kind of thinking in her response to Mr. Jordan:

> I saw a visitor from the state agricultural office who told me about a new pea seed which consistently germinates and grows to the same size each year. If we used this seed, we could do away with the grading steps after harvesting and freeze the peas in half the time.

Another approach to making thinking more productive and precise is advocated by Dr. A. Ellis in his book *A Guide to Rational Living*. He emphasizes the correction of mistaken beliefs through *rational* thinking. Note how each of the following irrational beliefs is based on unrealistic, illogical, inaccurate or overgeneralized thinking:

Irrational Beliefs About Meetings

- At the last meeting I received a lot of recognition. Therefore, surely it should happen again.
- This meeting will be an important test of my value to the organization. I must therefore always appear competent, making no errors.
- This meeting must live up to my expectations. If not, it's a poor meeting.

Irrational Beliefs About Others

- I want to be liked all the time for everything I do. If not, it's a dangerous sign that I am socially inadequate.
- Teammates seem to know much more about what's going on. Therefore, they must be *better* than I.
- If I don't get my needs satisfied at a meeting, I have failed —or the meeting has let me down.

Irrational Beliefs About Self

- I am judged as a useful member of the team even though I'm not well prepared and don't use much effort.
- If someone criticizes me or points out an error, it reduces my value as a person.
- If I did anything out of line—irrelevant or inappropriate—I should be blamed and punished.
- The leader represents the only real power and only his or her will is accomplished. My presence is insignificant.
- Lately, the leader seeks out my help. So, I keep giving the "expected" reactions.

Each one of the above statements represents an irrational belief. Each one of these beliefs leads to an emotional mix-up which interferes with clear thinking. This is illustrated by the case of J. Barnes who fears he's an outcast of the organization whenever he senses a lack of approval by other members of the team. When he tries to overcome this shattered image, he doesn't pay enough attention to the work of the meeting. To improve his thinking, J. has to identify his irrational belief.

For example, J. was crippled by self-doubts and fears when P. suggested, in a matter-of-fact tone, that one of J.'s recommendations exceeded the budgetary limit. J. seized upon this irrational conclusion: "If I didn't know such an obvious fact about our budget limits, I must be an idiot!"

Instead, J. should have come to the logical conclusion that forgetting even an obvious fact is a common human error. Often, a momentary distraction or lapse of concentration is the cause. Rarely, unless it's an oft-repeated occurrence, does it have anything to do with general ability as a team member.

Sensing and Feeling

If you're alive and breathing, you can *feel* and *sense*! Yet often you're warned to ignore sensing and feeling at meetings as though these skills don't belong. Perhaps, what is feared is not so much the use of these emotions but their abuse.

It's difficult to draw a line between feelings that are self-centered—which control you—and those which are modified and adapted to a situation—which *you* control. A loss of temper or a fit of uncontrolled laughter can be embarrassing—and if repeated, can grow to a sizable handicap. On the other hand, by delaying the expression of your feelings you have the chance to match them to your observations.

Sensitivity refers to the skill of getting to know others as they really are, to transmit this understanding, and to let others get to know you. Your senses and feelings are there waiting to inform you about people and situations. Sensitivity at a meeting enables you to evaluate and interpret correctly what others are saying and doing. With this understanding, you "wrap up" the experience by aiming messages clearly on target for the listener. Sensitivity can be built into your own style and become an important part of your functioning. The first step is to develop your powers of *intuition* and *empathy*.

Intuition. A sudden flash of awareness that leads to interpretations and solutions for actual situations and problems you encounter.

Empathy. The skill of getting *into*—not under—someone's skin, of *feeling* how he or she might be feeling. (However, at the same time, you're able to shuttle back to who you are and what you are experiencing.)

Opportunities for practicing these skills are all around us.

Jane K. used intuition and empathy to become an accurate judge of people. Usually she recognized: when others liked or disliked her; when they were trying to be right all the time; when they were being hostile in an uncontrolled, cold way, or when they were more constructively and aggressively advancing their own ideas and when the mood was cooperative and serious or when the members were resistive and inhibited.

Jane had achieved these intuitive gifts through long practice in observing others and then verifying the accuracy of her observations.

First, Jane uses her *senses* to perceive clearly what's being said and done. ("I see a person with a pad and a long list of carefully written statements.") She brings in her store of *knowledge and memories* to further her impressions. ("This person is well organized and plans in advance. His list, however, seems unnecessarily long and he seems determined to go over it point-by-point.") She keeps herself open to how she *feels* about people. ("I'm on edge because his fussiness makes me feel that I'm in his control, forced to sit here and listen to him drone on and on. I think I'll tell him that his efficient planning can serve as a model for all of us, but once we all agree on the broad outlines, he can follow through on the details on his own.")

By using her senses, her powers of thinking and feeling, Jane arrived at a short-cut, efficient impression. This gave her an accurate understanding of her teammate. During the meeting, Jane followed up her *intuition* with *empathy* to create a satisfying working relationship. She was able to identify with her teammate's fine qualities—and even acknowledge them verbally—while remaining true to her own needs and feelings.

Willing and Behaving

Your action at a meeting calls for selected kinds of *willing* and *behaving*. You may know, feel or sense what to do. But how do you translate these intentions into action? Or you may know how to do certain things at a meeting, but how do you carry them out consistently and skillfully?

Here are some techniques and strategies to turn your good intentions into actions.

"I"-Behavior

- Take "ownership" of your statements by using the word "I" instead of "we" or "us."

- Speak in the *here and now*. Don't get stuck in memories or references to past meetings or jump ahead to something that may occur later.

- Be selective about expressing your positive and negative feelings. Express sincerely what you are feeling, but temper it with your sensitivity to what is appropriate.

- Take every opportunity to improve your non-verbal manner. Relaxed, steady breathing will help you concentrate better than tapping your foot, slumping or staring into space.

- Remain self-aware but not self-centered. For the sake of group productivity, give up your "private agenda" and personal gratifications. The ultimate question to ask is: "Have I kept in sight the interests and needs of team, task and organization? Do I keep in mind that a meeting is not play, a battlefield, a family scene or a therapy session?"

"WE"-Behavior

- Realize that you're working with people who, like you, want to receive positive responses. Therefore, give them freely. When you do give negative feedback, your criticism will be accepted if it's expressed in a supportive and nonpunitive way.
- Assume that all team members' statements can be understood better. The more you check, the better the communication. Don't take for granted that everyone likes or dislikes, agrees or disagrees with what you've said. A brief question here and there keeps you accurately informed.
- Form working alliances with team members. But avoid forming sub-groups based on excluding others. This can only lead to the splitting and draining of valuable resources.
- Practice your leadership skills while you're a member if the leader of the meeting encourages such development. Promote a well-run meeting by joining in a review of the ongoing process whenever necessary.

"IT"-Behavior

- Remember the meaning and impact of the task as it was defined and addressed by participants at the start of the meeting. Let your own version of the task develop as the meeting proceeds. Listen to the ways others are pursuing the same task. Demonstrate your understanding of the task by supplementing, comparing or underlining these various views of the task.
- Enthusiasm and initiative in coping with the task separates the footdragging, passive member from the successful teammate. Not every meeting is fascinating, but resisting will not get it over faster.
- Planning and analyzing the issues in advance are skills too often neglected. You can germinate ideas which can develop and "hatch" at the meeting.

MEMO

SUBJECT: A meeting challenges you to be uniquely yourself as well as a working partner. You're called on to practice new psychological skills and to use old ones. Therefore, it's important to develop these skills and have them available.

1. Raise the level and power of your thinking by submitting it to tests like these: Are you making an effort to <u>concentrate</u> for longer periods of time? Are you drawing the right <u>conclusions?</u> Are you using your <u>memory</u> effectively? Do you avoid <u>irrational beliefs</u> about your <u>total</u> worth, based on rarely repeated common failings?

2. The meeting offers opportunities to practice, and be rewarded for, <u>sensitivity</u> (understanding the meaning of another's behavior), <u>intuition</u> (flashes of clear awareness) and <u>empathy</u> (having the same "vibrations").

3. Behavior has to be <u>willed</u> to carry out your good intentions and plans. <u>"I"-Behavior</u> consists of the most potent and influential ways of representing yourself. <u>"We"-Behavior</u> consists of the give-and-take with team members which marks you as useful and productive. <u>"It"-Behavior</u> describes the skills you can bring to the content and substance of the work and its procedures.

14:
We Are the Same-but Different

People at meetings who amuse, stimulate and work along with you are simply delightful. But there are always a few who are incompatible and have a distressing effect. They threaten, irritate or inhibit and plunge you into a turbulent sea of doubts and fears.

There are several familiar ways of controlling your reactions to the pressures of other members. Recall the lessons from childhood about fairness, tolerance and sportsmanship—the "rules of the game." They're not easy to carry out when the game is a complicated and serious assignment involving your ability and reputation. But exactly what can you do if you must work with someone who is incompatible?

Here is a three-stage procedure to help you deal effectively with "people problems." It consists of **awareness, decision** and **action.**

1. Become *aware* of what you see in the person who bothers or distresses you. (Is it really the way June keeps lists and files of everything—or is it that you're in awe of her efficiency?)

2. Make a *decision* whether this is a quality you reject or covet. (Don't say, "I never want to be like June; she's too organized," until you decide honestly whether or not you really dislike this quality.)

3. Take *action* by adopting part of this quality if you can make use of it; or take *action* by diverting—divert June from her list-making and redirect her into a more useful channel, as coordinator of follow-up projects, for example.

A Day at the Circus

Picture a circus and all its fascinating characters. In some ways, circus performers are strikingly similar to the types of people you encounter at a meeting. The Giant (a dominant talker); the Strong Man (a power-seeker); the Fat Lady (the one who takes it all in); the Midget (a self-effacer); the Siamese Twin (vacillating and self-contradicting); the Pinhead Boy (confused and uncomprehending); the Wild Man (impulsive and uncontrolled); the Trapeze Artist (a graceful exhibitionist); the Clown (lighthearted and humorous) and Assistant Ringmaster (member who constantly assists the leader).

Each of these types is grand entertainment at a circus—but each can cause great tension at a meeting. Each will be viewed through the eyes of a meeting member. Then you'll see how the use of the tools of *awareness, decision* and *action* can raise the level of performance at a meeting.

Introducing: The Giant.

Awareness: Edgar realizes the Giant wants to tower over, to be seen and heard, to lead the company in making sweeping changes.

Decision: Edgar thinks, *I'm feeling overwhelmed by the Giant's dominating behavior. I can't sit silently fuming. I've got to do something about it.*

Action: Edgar speaks out: "I've listened to what you (Giant) had to say. Now I'd like to add my observations. My information concerning our profits indicates we made the right decisions this quarter. Therefore, I don't agree with you (Giant) that radical changes are in order...."

Introducing: The Strong Man.

Awareness: Julie realizes the Strong Man wants to manipulate opinions to personal advantage; to gain power by absorbing four smaller departments into his own.

Decision: Julie thinks, *I'm not in favor of this kind of internal empire-building. And I'm irritated that someone from a higher rung of the organization (Strong Man) thinks he can take advantage by throwing his weight around. He should be using logic and leadership rather than sheer prestige to make his points. I'd like to use some of my own logic and muscle in a way that will get me some respectful notice.*

Action: Julie speaks out: "I believe it's important that we air everyone's opinions on this crucial topic. I, for one, don't see any rational reason for combining the departments. But couldn't we take a 10-minute break right now and talk in a more informal, relaxed way?"
Introducing: The Fat Lady.
Awareness: Annette realizes the Fat Lady craves safety; to be walled off from the world; to rest securely, to take it all in.
Decision: Annette thinks, *She (Fat Lady) reminds me that I'm too much on-the-go at meetings . . . always driving myself to say something . . . feeling that I have to make "important" contributions. But unlike the Fat Lady, I have no wall behind which to reflect and rest.*
Action: Annette decides: "I'll try to use meetings as opportunities to listen and benefit from the words and actions of others. I'll take in more and digest it all leisurely. I want to settle for a less hectic pace, behind a low but safe wall.
Introducing: The Midget.
Awareness: Doug understands that the Midget is like the child inside every adult. The "child" looks up to all the grown-ups at the meeting and feels unworthy. At meetings, Doug feels like giving up and going home when he can't think of any proposals to solve the task. He tries to gain sympathy by disparaging himself with comments like: "I'm no use to you. I've got nothing to offer today."
Decision: Doug thinks, *I must be careful not to allow the child in me to rule my behavior. At meetings, I let it happen. As a result, I invite everyone to join the game of "Step on Me."*
Action: Doug decides: Maybe I can't erase my stage fright at meetings. But at least I can concentrate on doing some things successfully. First, I can prepare by thinking over carefully what I want to say, to make sure it comes out of the competent side of me. And I can give my full and sympathetic attention to everyone.
Introducing: The Siamese Twin.
Awareness: The Siamese Twin goes in several directions at once. While saying one thing, his or her tone of voice or gesture means another. Tomas is in danger of becoming a "Siamese Twin": he thinks one way but feels another. At a recent meeting, he asked

three pertinent questions but prevented anyone from answering by darting off in another direction. Then he demanded angrily: "Why doesn't anyone address the issues?"

Decision: Tomas realizes: *I've been throwing out mixed signals. I've been afraid to risk committing myself to what I'm saying— to own my words and deeds. If I don't give full messages—not half-way and half-concealed ones—anger and frustration will be the result. It was the result at the last meeting. The Siamese Twin approach may be useful in diplomacy, politics and negotiation. But as a meeting member, my productivity is in direct proportion to the clarity and coherence of what I say.*

Action: Tomas decided: If I ask a question, not only must I wait for an answer, but I should listen to it, too. If there are two sides to an issue, and I lean toward one, I will state freely which side I am on—and why. I must break free of my "twin" and give clear and exact signals from now on.

Introducing: The Pinhead Boy.

Awareness: Gilbert understands that a Pinhead Boy is confused about the theme, purpose, or process of a meeting. When the leader announced, "Our profits dropped suddenly last quarter. This is a difficult situation and we've got to find ways of pulling ourselves up quickly," Gilbert gave in to despair and confusion. Blaming himself for the entire profit loss, he became demoralized. Feeling that the leader was pointing a finger directly at him, Gilbert locked his mind shut and prayed he'd be left alone.

Decision: Gilbert thinks, *I can't go around feeling like a pinhead, bowled over by the big ball. After all, a meeting is only an approximate way of dealing with complex problems of an organization. Still, it's the best we have. It's so easy to become skeptical, especially if I forget the team effort and take the full burden on my own shoulders.*

Action: Gilbert decides to speak out: When I feel burdened by guilt about my effectiveness at a meeting, I'm going to air these doubts. I bet I'll strike a common chord in others. Maybe they, too, feel that a finger's pointing at them. If so, we might join forces and make the meeting work better.

Introducing: The Wild Man.

Awareness: Fran understands that Bill is the Wild Man in her firm. He's full of strong impulses and feelings which, when expressed, come out as self-centered digressions. They destroy the discipline of a meeting. For instance, Fran was trying to concentrate on the task of how to word a company press release regarding an upcoming legal battle. But Bill began to rant and rave about the lawsuit and then about an incompatible next-door neighbor. The result was a disruptive distraction that got everyone off the track.

Decision: Fran realizes, *I, too, need an audience to share moods, gripes and troubles. But this is not the place for a rap session. The Wild Man in Bill must be reined in. If he won't do it; I will.*

Action: Fran speaks out: "Bill, we want to issue this statement to the press today. We have some difficult decisions before us. Ted, Nadine and I wrote up a first draft. I believe you have a copy. Suppose you save your personal comments for lunch and give us your input on our position paper. We'd like to hear your thoughts on this."

Introducing: The Trapeze Artist.

Awareness: Alex understands that Nelson is a Trapeze Artist in that he takes chances gracefully—sometimes at considerable risk. Nelson's approach to a meeting is unique; he has an original flair. But when he brings in unusual facts and cleverly pulls together opinions, Alex sits numb with awe and envy.

Decision: Alex realizes, *Looking with awe, envy or disdain at a good performer won't help me to use my own tools properly. I'm not a showman but I do need—and enjoy—applause.*

Action: Alex decides to prepare to change. He knows that success at a meeting *does* require performing. He decides to himself: I can make myself more interesting and likable. I'll pay more attention to my delivery. I can't expect to perform well unless I deliver well.

Introducing: The Clown.

Awareness: Rex understands that a Clown makes us laugh at ourselves. At a meeting a clown can relieve the grimness. But sometimes, Rex's clowning becomes a foolish diversion. More than once, it has led to his own misgivings about wasted time as well as the disapproval of management.

Decision: Rex knows, *If I keep it under control, I can serve an* *important purpose by releasing energy and putting the meeting into a better perspective.*

Action: Rex decides: I have a talent; I can lighten the spirit of a meeting. I'd like to contribute my ability to draw others into better working relationships. But I must remember that too much clowning is seen as "fooling around." I'll have to limit my light-heartedness to appropriate moments only, by developing greater sensitivity to the mood of the meeting.

Introducing: The Assistant Ringmaster.

Awareness: Crosby would like to learn more leadership skills. But when he sees Jackson offering to help adjust the ventilation and seating at one meeting, and Sommers reminding the leader about absentees at another meeting, he becomes inwardly resentful.

Decision: Crosby realizes, *If I want to learn more about how to lead, I have no justification for criticizing someone who is trying to do the same.*

Action: Crosby decides: I, too, will help run the meeting. Since I'm interested in the inner workings of a meeting, I'll begin by offering my help with meeting maintenance.

Skills for Awareness, Decision and Action

Here are the skills you need to carry out *awareness, decision* and *action* in your teamwork.

To gain *awareness* of other people, pay special attention to what is going on directly before you. Use all your senses to get impressions. How does the leader sound and look? Listen carefully to what each member is saying. Get in touch with your feelings.

Decision skills are used to determine whether you want to be more like, less like, closer or more distant to someone. Look at your own goals and values. Then decide what you require from the other person and how much of an accommodation you're willing to make to get it.

Taking *action* means fulfilling your powers as a group member in concert with others on the team. The skills needed include: The ability to speak for yourself directly, clearly and responsibly; the ability to channel your feelings into helpful feedback; the taking of risks by reaching out even before you know if you'll be accepted; the verifying of your impressions with the other's behavior.

> # MEMO
>
> SUBJECT: An awareness of the wide range of personality types helps you correct or improve certain characteristics in yourself and encourage fuller development and usefulness in others.
>
> At meetings you encounter many figures from the human circus: The Giant, the Strong Man, the Fat Lady, the Midget and a host of others. Once you identify them, make productive use of your reactions with this three-stage procedure:
>
> 1. First, when you get a negative signal about someone, try to become <u>aware</u> of what specific qualities distress you.
>
> 2. Then <u>decide</u>: Are these qualities which you admire and wish to bring out within yourself—or is it necessary for you to oppose or resist them for the sake of the meeting?
>
> 3. Then <u>act</u> on your decision by assuming control over your reactions to influence other members.

15:
"I Said, You Said..."

In this chapter, a close-up view of productive responses by members at a centered meeting is presented. The task is passed from one hand to another, developed and improved by participants in their own unique, chosen ways.

Each response helps build the task in one of three directions:
- **Cultivating.** The speaker expedites the pace and direction of the meeting along a steady path to the goal. Includes: Initiating, giving and receiving information. Also, establishing agreement on what has been decided so far.
- **Experimenting.** The speaker introduces a broadening, heightening or deepening quality to the task. Includes: Following the ground rules in a more daring, untested way.
- **Weeding.** The speaker modifies or eliminates what has been said because it is irrelevant or repetitious. Includes: Getting back to the thread of the meeting by clarifying, summarizing and expanding on it.

Background of Meeting

The Universal Airlines Company has been shaken by several major upheavals. Important replacements were made in the top level of management. And Universal has expanded by buying out two smaller airlines. There is widespread uncertainty and speculation about new policies, job security and the recent drop in earnings. There has been a loss in efficiency and productivity at all levels.

The CEO (Chief Executive Officer) gave high priority to improving morale in the company. He decided to reach into the rich resources of the company and elicit a self-directed effort—a kind of "floating task group"—on the problem of morale. Members were selected from various divisions and staffs.

Those Attending

Mr. Mathews (M). Age 56. Divisional Manager (Maintenance), directly under the President. Supervision and administration of engineers and mechanics. Self-made man who fled Europe after World War II. Authoritarian, yet friendly and sensitive.

Mr. Gorham (G). Age 42. Personnel Director in charge of hiring and training. Discussion leader of this task group. Well liked and respected for his ideas about the human factor in organizations. Has created ideas which at times are called "impractical."

Ms. West (W). Age 27. Flight Attendant. Energetic. Deals surprisingly well with the public even though shy and self-effacing.

Ms. Sorrenti (S). Age 39. Office manager at headquarters office. In charge of clerical and accounting personnel. A rather demanding supervisor. Tends to placate those above her.

Mr. Peters (P). Age 22. Ticket agent. Facile and bright. Has a theatrical manner. Tends to buckle under pressure at busy times.

Mr. Timkin (T). Age 42. Assistant to advertising manager. A practical "doer." Enjoys the excitement of new leads and competition. Prefers definite problems and concrete solutions.

Mr. Hardy (H). Age 45. Purchasing Manager, head of purchasing office. Closely resembles the "self-actualizing" person who has achieved balance, wisdom and rich personal and social achievement. Uses energy adaptively rather than impressing others with façades, defenses and manipulations.

As the Meeting Begins

Bill Gorham, the personnel director, is assigned leader. He has already met with the group to brief them on the method of *centering*. The agreed-upon theme is: "Morale-Building for Person, Personnel and Company."

Members arrive from different parts of the building and city. Ms. West is a few minutes late because her incoming flight was delayed. Mr. Mathews left a message that he might be delayed at a conference, but arrives in time. The seats are arranged in a circle in the conference room. The mood is relaxed and somewhat expectant.

NOTE: These are excerpts from the first hour of a two-hour meeting. The dialogue is in the left-hand column. The right-hand column analyzes the productive impact of the speakers, according to the *cultivating, experimenting* or *weeding* direction of their words.

In addition, labels are included for figure-ground combinations (chapter 8). The first word of the pair refers to the foreground of the response; the second word, to the background. TASK always will appear in the foreground or background in combination with I (member), WE (team), IT (work element) or ORGANIZATION. So, "TASK-WE" means task in front focus with team awareness in background.

The Universal Airlines Company
Task-Theme: Morale-Building for Person, Personnel and Company

WHAT WAS SAID	PRODUCTIVE IMPACT
1. G: (Slightly amused) I was no more surprised than you when the CEO called me in for this assignment. I still feel tension because Universal sure dropped a heavy load on me—and on us.	1. **Cultivating.** In being himself —*self-stating*—G. aims for symmetry with others. He serves as a model of candor. By giving up the rigid leader's role, he can be more patient and sensitive to the work-styles of members. (I-TASK)
2. T: (Shaking his head) It's going to take more than just this project to fix what's wrong with the whole company.	2. **Experimenting.** In a kind of *confrontation*, he makes a good, practical point. He *widens* the discussion to include others in the company. (ORGANIZATION-TASK)

WHAT WAS SAID	PRODUCTIVE IMPACT
3. G: Sure, other things are being done. There's a weekly bulletin on new developments in the company. And people in my office have been working on the morale problem. We're updating some of those good recommendations we made last year.	3. **Cultivating.** By *responding factually* he agrees that it is important for others in the company to be involved. (IT-TASK)
4. T: (Smiling) This is begininng to look good. Our inside view would certainly give a lot of people concrete leads about morale in the company.	4. **Cultivating.** In an *encouraging* way, he arouses enthusiasm by showing the importance of the team task. (TASK-WE)
5. G: (Looking around at everyone) Sure, that's what the CEO thought, too. By the way, we can give him results in any form we choose.	5. **Cultivating.** With this *information-giving*, he underlines the importance of the job from the top management's view. (ORGANIZATION-TASK)
6. M: This reminds me of some other jobs I've been given, where the goals seem to be at the horizon, somewhere. But the difference here is that I can feel people really pulling together.	6. **Cultivating.** *Associates* task to a past experience. Also pulls group together by *reaching out* to pull together. (TASK-I)
7. W: (Turning to Peters) This week I was wondering why *I* was picked—to be with managers and others from all over the company.	7. **Cultivating.** *Relating* to another person directly. *Reaches out* for a "we" feeling by revealing initial discomfort with higher level members. (I-TASK)
8. S: (Looking at Gorham) I'd like to take better aim at the point of this meeting. You told us that the focus was "morale."	8. **Weeding.** Minimizing a *previous comment*. A successful attempt to deal with the higher priority of getting to the wording of a Task-Theme. (TASK-IT)
9, 10, 11, 12, 13, 14. (Participants looked at the task or theme in their own ways—each showing a special interest in one or more particular aspects.)	9-14. **Cultivating.** Members arrive at *a consensus* on the task-theme: "Morale-building for person, personnel and company." (WE-TASK)

WHAT WAS SAID	PRODUCTIVE IMPACT
15. P: My morale needs a lot of approval. When I worked in theater before I started here, I could just taste that applause. When I pleased everyone at once, I was OK. Otherwise I felt like a nothing. At the airlines ticket counter, when there are more than three on line, forget it. I get jumpy and begin to hate my job. I guess I need a lot of what they call "stroking" to put on a good performance.	15. **Cultivating.** His *sharing* of a personal dilemma encourages others to do the same. Secondly, he *narrows* the theme, which permits him to make a solid addition to task-solving. (I-TASK)
16, 17, 18, 19, 20, 21, 22, 23. (Participants continue talking about what best sustains their morale at work. Some of the examples given were shown to be exaggerated expectations.)	16-23. **Weeding.** Several members asked others to *restrict* their comments, which were taking up excessive meeting time—comments which emphasized unrealistic demands for support and gratification on the job. (TASK-I)
24. G: I remember a favorite fairy tale about a band of people. One was very tall, another had telescopic eyes, a third was very powerful, and so forth. And then I looked at all of you, each with striking differences. I guess I'm thinking of how people can complement each other, each with different gifts.	24. **Experimenting.** This piquant example is an attempt at *heightening* the level of the meeting through using an imaginative device. (WE-TASK)
25. H: That's what I've always aimed for—to be my own person, but also to have open channels for letting in the next person. I don't know what the CEO had in mind about this floating task group, but when this is over, I hope I'll have shared with all of you how morale works with real people, and not just statistics.	25. **Experimenting.** By announcing his own intentions he seems to be inviting the team members to think about teamwork more *deeply*. (WE-TASK)

WHAT WAS SAID	PRODUCTIVE IMPACT
26. T: What you just said, Hardy, rings a bell for me. After a certain point, when people don't feel involved, they begin to feel like kids under an "adult" management. As children, they start competing and wasting a lot of energy. (Still talking to Hardy, in a louder voice) You spoke about "real people." Work reviews, when they come, don't tell enough of what's really good and bad. I'll admit I make the same mistake when it comes to periodic ratings with my staff in advertising. I'm probably carrying on the same system that I'm under.	26. **Cultivating.** Feels free to *connect* to previous speaker and to *develop* further what was said. He *brings out more facts* about decision-making of employees which are directly on target for the theme of the meeting. (TASK-IT)
27-35. (Members gave examples of morale problems at work. Leader looked beyond this to focusing on solutions.)	27-35. **Weeding.** A *turnaround* of the direction of discussion from the way it was going. With this change of pace, G asked members to drop talk of what's wrong and concentrate on morale solutions. (TASK-IT)
36. G: (Looking toward Mathews) Never having been any good in math, I've looked up to engineers with awe. Your care and precision is so far from my style—which is to plunge into one situation after another. You just called my attention to a systematic answer, that is, to begin with, we must look for growth, achievement, responsibility and recognition. These are the bricks we can use to build morale.	36. **Experimenting.** *Interpreting or uncovering* someone else's behavior must be done tactfully. Here, Gorham succeeded in doing so. This led the meeting into deeper waters, opening up other channels of communication. (IT-TASK)

Productive Blips

On the radar screen of any meeting, three kinds of productive *blips* may be seen. The first, *cultivating*, was described in the preceding illustration as a response which nudges ahead the member, team or task at a steady pace. The second, *experimenting*, moves the member, team or task in longer leaps by probing more deeply or by making comments which widen or heighten the discussion. Third, is *weeding*, a way of thinning out extraneous or irrelevant comments. This classification is designed to give you a wider repertoire of responses—to help you decide what to say and when to come out with it.

Keys to *cultivating* from the illustration above may be seen in the following responses:
1. Self-stating.
3. Responding factually.
4. Encouraging.
5. Information-giving.
6. Associates task to a past experience; reaches out to pull members together.
7. Relating directly with words and movement to another.
9-14. Arriving at a consensus.
15. Sharing a personal dilemma.
26. Connecting or linking with a previous speaker.

Keys to *experimenting* may be seen in the following responses:
2. A) Confronting and disagreeing, if necessary.
   B) Widening and implying that there is much more than meets the eye.
24. Heightening through the use of imagination, metaphor or other venturesome moves.
25. Deepening with a daring concept or abstraction.
36. Interpreting or uncovering a member's behavior so the team's process can result in increased channels of communication.

Keys to *weeding* may be seen in the following responses:
8. Minimizing another's comment.
16-23. Restricting what is said to prevent the meeting from wandering down the path of unrealistic proposals.
27-35. Turnaround showing that a change of pace and direction are needed.

MAKING THE CONTENT COUNT

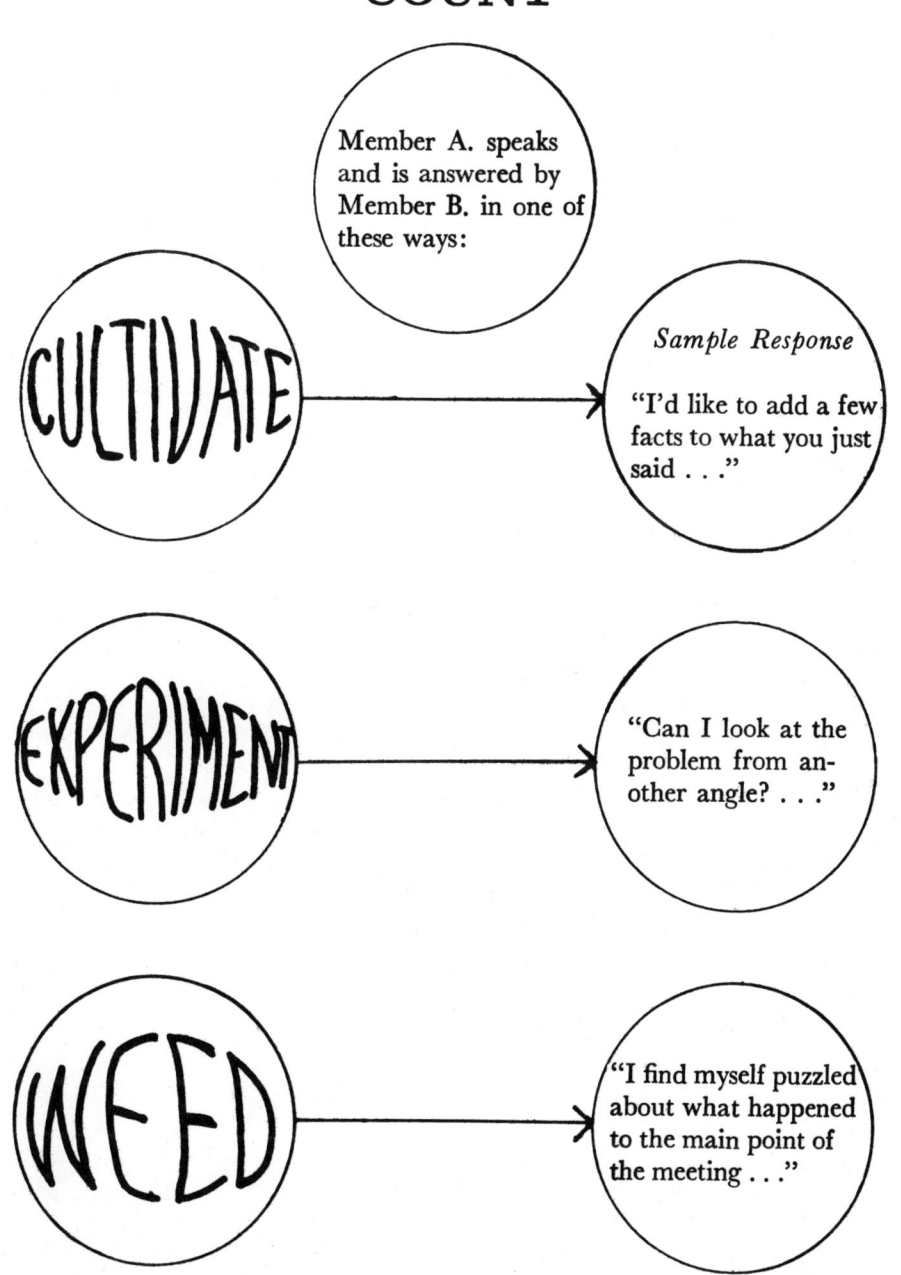

Member A. speaks and is answered by Member B. in one of these ways:

CULTIVATE

Sample Response

"I'd like to add a few facts to what you just said..."

EXPERIMENT

"Can I look at the problem from another angle?..."

WEED

"I find myself puzzled about what happened to the main point of the meeting..."

MEMO

SUBJECT: A close-up view of the transcript of a meeting can show all the important ingredients that go into the making of precise, economical and productive comments by participants.

1. You can <u>cultivate</u> by expediting the pace and direction of a meeting along a steady path.

2. You can <u>experiment</u> by introducing a broadening, heightening or deepening quality.

3. You can <u>weed</u> by modifying or eliminating an irrelevant or repetitious remark of a previous speaker.

16:
How to Shape a Meeting

In general, meetings have much in common since they all include communicating, producing, teaching and learning, with concern for task and people. But they can also be classified differently according to the predominant goals. The leader can then select the best format for the particular goal as the most efficient way of conducting the meeting.

These brief descriptions of types of meetings will each be followed by an account of how they are carried out in practice.

1. Presenting and Sharing Information.
Members of an organization must be kept informed and up-to-date on plans, developments, surveys—all the necessary data that go with efficiency and productivity.

2. Problem-Solving and Decision-Making.
The most common, if not the most complex, of meetings is where a change in ideas or action of the organization is called for to improve or increase its products or profits.

3. Creating New Ideas.
Members are asked to come up with new ideas and procedures which have not been thought of or used before.

4. Teaching and Training.
New skills and knowledge are often required by the changing needs of an organization. Or new members need orientation and training to augment the qualifications they bring with them.

Information Meeting

Your reaction to attending a well-run Information Meeting might be, "They think I'm important enough to give me the chance to ask questions and offer opinions." Your goal at this meeting is: not to *read about* information, or *hear about* it, but to become part of the *transmission*. A live exchange helps you absorb and use the data for your own—and the company's—benefit.

The Information Meeting is also the choice format for bringing in experts. Here, they can present material of a timely and relevant nature. As an outcome, you feel reassured that you've had the same exposure to the subject as everyone else—that you share in a common body of knowledge.

The *centered* approach provides useful techniques for the Information Meeting by emphasizing nailing down a central theme and staying with it. *Sharing* and active *listening*—intrinsic to the centered approach—helps you to succeed in a quietly effective way.

The Information Leader Makes It Work

The leader structures the meeting rather firmly to avoid going beyond the presentation and sharing of information. In effect, he or she says: "Let's go over the ground, get the facts, answer the questions and develop an understanding of what all this means for our work." To accomplish this, the leader asks members to be sure of the facts they are presenting, with emphasis on clarity of presentation.

Problem-Solving Meeting

You are often in the position of solving problems by trial and error, planning, coping and adapting. At meetings, problem-solving is also a widely used answer to doubt, confusion and indecision—producing resolution and change. In groups, this approach becomes more complicated as it draws upon communicating and compromising while also advancing your own ideas.

While there are many ways of solving problems at meetings, there is one particularly effective way which derives from the scientific method and its stages in the discovery of facts. These stages are: Problem, Goal, Evaluation and Solution, Decision-Making and Application.

The Problem-Solving Leader Makes It Work

The problem-solving stages are illustrated in a meeting of managers and assembly line workers of the tractor division of Acorn Machines. There has been a significantly high incidence of accidents and absences. Many of the employees are late to work. Linked to this is a suspicion that there is a rise in the problem of alcoholism among workers.

Acorn Tractor Division Meeting (Stages in Problem-Solving)

1. Problem. What's wrong? How did it happen? Get different views and perceptions of the problem. In this way, it becomes more clearly defined.

In this exploratory phase of the meeting it was brought out that the manual operations for the workers on the assembly line was unusually narrow and repetitive. Positions among the crew rarely were shifted since those who had the slightly more favorable operations held onto them.

The task-theme that was formulated, "Making People Count For More," reflected the company's awareness that mechanization was affecting efficiency and health adversely. This theme served as a springboard for further discussions about working conditions. A connection was made between the assembly line conditions and the problem raised by management regarding accidents and absences.

This was a fruitful start which led easily to the next phase.

2. Goal. How do you want things to be when free of the problem? Establish the goal or the way you want things to turn out.

It was agreed that something had to be done to reduce the boredom, absenteeism and other associated conditions, such as alcoholism. Reducing the incidences at least to the lower levels of the other divisions at Acorn was imperative.

This phase was easily accomplished since there was complete agreement about what had to be corrected and about the ill effects both on the workers and on the company.

3. Evaluation and Solution. What are the answers? Which one fits best? Arrive at the best solution through evaluation and, preferably, by consensus.

The leader asked members to decide on what criteria to use for the solutions to make the list more manageable. The main standard agreed upon was that the solution should aim for permanence and not be just a "band-aid."

Several answers were proposed: A. Piped-in music would make the time seem to go faster. B. More frequent visits by the chief engineer would make workers feel that they were no longer the "lost division." C. An extra break in mid-afternoon might be refreshing. D. A redesign of some operations would allow several people to work together as a broader unit.

Since each of the alternatives had its proponents, the leader asked for statements from everyone about what they liked or disliked about each. After this, the leader asked for a listing of solutions in order of preference. The first choice was solution D. In the discussion, one member reminded the others that most of the machines were easily movable and could be repositioned. Solution B was weakened when it was pointed out that the only result observed from the chief engineer's recent visit was that the men perked up for a moment—but felt no happier overall.

4. Decision-Making and Application. Has the decision been made appropriately—by consensus, vote, or by agreement to let the leader make a final determination? Is the solution solid enough to go ahead with a definite course of action? When, where, by whom?

The decision in the above case, fortunately, had a firm foundation. Several heads nodded in agreement when it was proposed to broaden and vary the operations of the production workers. The chief engineer, who was present at the meeting, volunteered to change the design of the production line. The leader said he'd recommend this proposal to the vice-president of the division, who originally raised the problem.

Another recommendation was made for a follow-up procedure. In six months, the personnel director must provide figures to determine the success of the plan. These figures will compare absentee records, medical files and accident statistics for this division, before and after the changes were made.

Creative Meetings

Centering is ideally suited for the Creative Meeting because of its emphasis on the way people can become more adventurous in bringing new ideas into existence. Even if some organizations survive in a fossil state, most others stay alive by continuously developing new possibilities and approaches to their product or service.

Virtually every one of the original ground rules is geared to creativity. The leader encourages the flow of material from members—giving birth to new combinations of thought and novel ways of using diverse talents. The task-theme, with its open-ended and flexible qualities, invites self-probing to evoke initiative, imagination and intuition.

It's doubtful that a Creative Meeting will make everyone automatically a creative person. But it could certainly bring out hidden possibilities. Developing creative skills is a lifelong project. It involves shaping your wide range of raw intellectual and artistic powers to create original products of good quality. Solutions range from structuring an organization in a new way to figuring out more uses for a toothpick; from photographing new facets of human behavior to composing a symphony.

A Creative Meeting is also the best way of putting together the work of people from various departments, disciplines or skills into new correlations and combinations. This is an example.

In a large, voluntary teaching hospital with an excellent reputation, one of the weak links in helping patients recover smoothly was the quality of the food service. Not one patient or doctor disagreed. As a result, patients' families resorted to a nineteenth century procedure of bringing in bags and baskets of nourishing, tasty and appropriate foods from the outside. This was done not without resentment by patient and family, however. The hospital administration was powerless to correct the situation.

Now imagine a scenario for a Creative Meeting, including the following: Head dietician, chief nurse, resident physician, staff gastroenterologist, hospital administrator, kitchen orderly and a recent patient. Each participant is asked to toss out ideas that arise spontaneously. The task of the meeting is to substitute fresh ideas for the stale ones. For example, several ideas put together yields: A mobile food cart run by a dietician during the one-hour meal periods for supplements, substitutions and additions to the diet.

This idea, when polished and formulated with care, can then be submitted to the hospital administration for follow-up. Then a Problem-Solving meeting with selected personnel would be organized to expedite the plan.

The Creative Meeting Leader Makes It Work

As the most flexible and free-flowing of all meetings, the creative type has the least formal structure. Nevertheless, there are guidelines to be followed. They include pre-planning, the opening, agreeing on ground rules and formulation of task-theme. Toward the end, the leader can ask for a review and a list of those ideas which emerged as most useful. Then combinations of these ideas could be considered.

As leader, you make it possible for each member to gather his or her thoughts about the subject of the meeting and to bounce them off others without feeling hurried or harassed. Members are given the freedom to develop those ideas which seem most valuable. One of those ideas will "click" louder than the others. Then it can be polished and verified with other members of the team.

Teaching and Training Meetings

Teaching is not like inducing a chemical reaction: It is much more like painting a picture or making a piece of music . . . planting a garden or writing a friendly letter . . . It cannot all be done by formulas, or you will spoil your work . . .—Gilbert Highet.

Until recently, knowledge, skills and attitudes were transmitted chiefly through families and apprenticeships—and to some extent through formal schools and teachers. Today there is much more emphasis on formal training.

Organizations are in the business of teaching, learning, training and reviewing. Older members have to learn new tricks to keep up or advance. New members have to learn old tricks to build their careers, as well as to demonstrate their value to the organization. The Teaching and Training Meeting is limited to learning and reviewing technical and other skills required for the success of the organization. Decision-making, exploring new information and creativity are not essential to the aims of this meeting.

There are specific benefits to members stemming from the Teaching Meeting which are:

* Opportunity of mastering facts about the work without having to extract the information through less direct or available channels.

* A good informal transition to, or relief from, the more taxing, formal aspects of the organization.
* An introduction to learning the skills of good discussion, decision-making and compromise.
* Communication training.
* Becoming a part of the organization by meeting others.

The Teaching and Training Leader Makes It Work

Teaching leaders have at their command the three main principles of good teaching: Prepare, Share and Reinforce. When these three principles are applied properly, it's almost impossible not to have a productive meeting.

Prepare. Your first requirement is to have a plan of what you intend to teach—a plan which encompasses not only the first few minutes of the meeting, but of the entire scope of the meeting. Otherwise, you may wind up with a brilliant two-minute opening followed by an hour of boredom and disorganization.

The best lecturers, trainers and teaching leaders prepare their materials carefully. They know how they are going to introduce their material, they know most of the questions that'll be asked, and they know how much information to give. The more smoothly it goes, the more they have probably prepared. Even if you have done it many times before, bring your material up to date, review the backgrounds of your audience and check your notes and demonstration materials.

If you keep only one step ahead of members, you'll deprive them of what they need to know. Your poorly memorized data or the narrow scope of what you have remembered accurately will only water down what they really came for. Not to mention what will be thought of *your* performance. (And remember: A performance it is. An actor would never go on stage without knowing his lines letter-perfect. Neither should you!)

If you do not like the subject you are presenting, this may be unfortunate but unavoidable. Sometimes you simply must deal with unappealing material. But if you express boredom and disinterest, expect your audience to lose interest themselves—a fatal disease in any learning situation. They will say you are efficient, that you "know your stuff" and have a good sense of humor. But they will emerge from the meeting with a feeling of disappointment in the final product—what they've actually learned.

Share. As Teaching Leader you not only profess your knowledge and skill but also share it by communicating clearly and effectively.

First, this can be done by finding out in advance, or on the spot, what the members know or don't know about the subject or procedure to be mastered. This avoids wasting time in telling them what they already know.

Second, you have several time-proven methods of presentation at your disposal which can be used alone or in combination. *Lecturing* is the best choice when you have an organized body of facts that notes or books could not duplicate. *Asking questions* enables you to help members build knowledge from something they already know in part. *Discussing* is best when members already know something about the subject and you want to explain it more fully.

Third, in sharing, you must maintain a generous and fair attitude. Even that good but harsh teacher you remember fondly from childhood, who worked you so hard, tried to use fairness while being strict.

Apart from fairness, a rather tight rein must be kept on the whole teaching-learning-training process. Without this, the natural tendency of most learners to avoid the difficult and new, will result in a slackening of effort. This requires that you take strong leadership from start to finish. At the start you state firmly what you expect will be learned. During the meeting you keep up a state of tension and motivation by directing glance and word to members who seem to be faltering. Give frequent summaries to indicate not only how much has been done but what still remains.

Reinforce. Since the Teaching Meeting aims primarily at changing or improving behavior, the learning has to be strengthened and fixed to make it last. Contrary to the methods of lion-tamers, humans learn best with praise and encouragement. Leaders easily can lose sight of the fact that the child within even hardened adults responds appreciatively to recognition and acceptance.

Further along on the spectrum of reinforcement are challenges to members. An informal contest or quiz will cause a member to galvanize his attention and concentration on the task.

For each kind of learning or training, an effective leader has his or her own technique for reinforcing the material and making it stick:

- At training sessions involving machinery upkeep, one instructor had a clever way of "bugging" the sample machines in advance to demonstrate a flaw caused by poor upkeep. Members were reinforced by carrying into successful practice what they had learned from the manual and discussion.
- At a meeting to train food handlers in the intricacies of governmental regulations, the leader divided the meeting into two teams. He acted as the governmental inspector and shot questions at each team to compare how they would fare in an actual inspection.
- At a management training session, the leader prepared a case history of a typical personnel problem. After getting answers to multiple choice questions, she showed how each answer could be scored according to five categories of management style. Members were stimulated to observe their own and others' tendencies toward having a consistent style as manager.

SHAPING A MEETING

What Has to Be Done	How It Should Be Done	The Form It Takes
The Goal, Task or Theme	Transmitting and digesting information	Presenting and Sharing
	Solving problems, dilemmas and issues	Problem-Solving
	Constructing novel combinations of ideas. Seeing the same idea in a new context	Creating New Ideas
	Providing orientation, teaching and training	Teaching and Learning

MEMO

SUBJECT: The medium of the meeting determines its message.

1. While meetings have much in common, they take on different shapes. These include: Presenting and Sharing Information, Problem-Solving and Decision-Making, Creating New Ideas, and Teaching and Training. Each of these formats requires a different emphasis in procedure.

2. The Information leader holds the reins firmly while exploring the terrain.

3. The Problem-Solving leader makes sure to follow a sequence of steps from definition to application.

4. The Creative leader is on a search for new combinations of ideas and thoughts by challenging members to reach into their hidden and unused powers.

5. The Teaching and Training leader uses a method tested and proven by the great teachers. The <u>plan</u> is the curriculum which includes the body of knowledge to be transmitted. This must be <u>shared</u> with members in a way that recognizes their state of knowledge and readiness to receive it. Then there is <u>practice</u> and <u>review</u> for reinforcement.

17:
Stimulating Productivity

A properly run meeting has "automatic pilot" mechanisms allowing it to hum along unpiloted for short periods of time. Under the right conditions, a meeting grows by itself. From time to time you can lean back and enjoy this happening.

At most other times you're busy planning, directing and instructing. On occasion a leader might ask for a *demonstration interaction exercise*. This will interrupt the ongoing process and pace so, despite its potential value, the interaction exercise should be used with caution.

Before introducing such a change—even if it is a brief interlude—first make certain that the exercise is needed to make an important improvement in the way members are working. Secondly, these exercises should be done sparingly to avoid giving members the impression that they will be bailed out of a momentary snag by the "all-seeing, all-knowing" leader.

Many such devices are used without being considered an "exercise." For example, it is a common practice for a leader to go around the room and ask everyone to introduce themselves. Another practice is to ask members to change seats or realign chairs to free an oppressively formal atmosphere and to introduce fresh relationships.

Four such exercises follow. Several of them have been adapted from the National Training Laboratory materials. And there's no reason why you can't devise some exercises of your own. Just make sure they're based on the nature of the organization, the content of the meeting and the readiness of participants to engage in something involving an element of surprise and risk.

Exercises in Productivity

- Brainstorming
- "Johari Window"
- Small Group Work
- Style of Teamwork

Brainstorming

Purpose: To illustrate the value of creative and spontaneous thinking in meetings. To encourage risk-taking as a way of becoming involved in productive work.

Technique: At an early stage, select an area of the task and ask members to toss out as many ideas as they can. Example: "What must be done about supertanker accidents to preserve our oceans in the next decade?" The recorder writes down the ideas. No comments or criticisms are permitted. But the leader is free to encourage answers when there is faltering. The leader then asks the assistance of members to identify the five or 10 most useful clusters of ideas. These then become the springboard for further discussion.

Outcome: (1) Provides a relatively safe shared activity in the beginning of the meeting. (2) Is a useful way to center the task while also working with variations in the way others perceive the task. (3) Is a good way to provide an initial exploration and definition of the task.

"Johari Window"

You are different from others in the degree of knowing and revealing yourself. This is illustrated in J. Luft's "Johari Window" (*Human Relations Training News*, 1961) as a window with four different panes. In one area you know a certain part of yourself and can share this. In the second, you know a part of yourself but conceal it. In the third, you're blind to a part of yourself but let it out. (Example: You act aggressively but declare: "I'm not angry at all!") In the fourth, you carry an unknown part of yourself which is too deeply imbedded to be recognized by you or observed by others.

Purpose: To admit more "light" so you can see yourself and others more clearly, promoting better understanding and communication. Open the "window" by encouraging mild confrontations.

Technique: At a point when members have developed good working relationships but where an increase in mutual understanding is required to advance the meeting, the leader steps in. (1) Leader asks members to look around and decide what it is they want to say about the behavior of any other member. (2) Each in turn says: "The thing that puzzles me most about you is . . ." or "The thing I want to tell you most is . . ." (3) The member addressed has the choice of discussing this comment with the person who made it. (4) After this brief interchange, they should request the reactions of the others.

Outcome: The areas of light will become enlarged. The blind spots will be decreased and the façade will be lowered.

Small Group Work

Purpose: To give each team member a more active role by practicing participation in a small group.

Technique: At any point in a meeting, the leader announces that members usually get a better chance to express themselves in a small group. Ask the entire group to form into units of four or five. Present the groups with their assignments—which may either be the same or vary from group to group. Example of a common assignment: "Which one of the various solutions to the traffic jam in the cafeteria do you favor, and why?"

After 15 minutes, the small groups are asked to reassemble. Ask one member of each sub-group to give a five-minute report to the whole team on what was significant for him or her during the small meeting. As the general meeting continues, members may refer to the new material which has been generated.

Outcome: (1) Creates a change of pace which will bring members closer together and enhance participation. (2) Gives an opportunity for a leadership role to the reporters. (3) The subdividing and reuniting demonstrate the possibilities ultimately for keeping the team together.

Style of Teamwork

Purpose: To illustrate what different members of a team can offer.

Technique: After the meeting has been going for at least a half-hour explain that members have different qualities in teamwork which aren't readily identified or used.

Ask adjoining members to face each other as couples. For the next five to 10 minutes allow A to give impressions of B as a team member—positive or negative. A should relate to B on a one-to-one basis. Then reverse the procedure, with B telling A. (This can take the form of an interview in which a member asks questions to check his or her observations. However, it should be made clear that these are only subjective impressions.)

Reassemble the team and ask for those willing to have a partner/member reveal some of the observations.

Outcome: Members learn how they are perceived as team members. Hearing both positive and negative comments, they become less sensitive to criticism or praise.

The Play in Meetings

A sharp line is usually drawn between serious meetings and play. Yet the expression, "To play around with an idea" has a place in the most serious surroundings. The previous exercises obviously suggest a form of play.

When you take a close look at the unique elements of both play and a *centered* meeting, you find ways in which you can use the freedom and excitement of play to advance the progress of a "serious" meeting.

Listen for the echoes of play at a meeting and it will become possible to join in ways suggested by J. Huizinga (*Homo Ludens*) with your own playing skills.

- Stepping out of "ordinary life": The common ground rules represent a game aspect with its own rules. Ordinary habits of communication cluttered by caution and fear can be suspended.
- There is a special order created by the ground rules which brings a temporary, limited form of wholeness and perfection in the way they work.
- The procedures invite risking a give-and-take of ideas. At the

same time each member's prowess, courage and tenacity is tested by having to stick to the rules.
- As with play, often a meeting has the power to extend itself after it is over. The lure and spirit of a meeting extend to its members beyond its formal completion.
- The centered meeting encourages each member to take imaginative and creative positions—which becomes a sort of "dressing up," as in play.
- Play is a contest for representing something in the best possible way by temporarily stepping out of ordinary life. The shaping of task into theme is also a way of representing the assignment in a better—more perfect—way by enlarging it and relating it to the people doing the task.

Managing Conflict

Productive leaders don't shy away from conflict whether it be over personal, procedural, factual or team issues. Some clashes take the form of good-natured teasing and confronting, which are not destructive. But other collisions between members can be disagreeable and counterproductive. Even so, such conflicts can be reprocessed into enthusiasm, cohesiveness and into a raised level of thinking. The most successful formula to accomplish this is recognizing the conflict and then diverting it. There are several such approaches by the leader:

1. Ask for more facts. The act of uncovering additional information may in itself defuse the conflict.

2. Spot the areas of agreement which may have eluded those members in conflict. When this is called to their attention they are relieved by the chance to back off gracefully.

3. Dilute the personality clash by asking for ideas from others.

4. As another diversion, request a change of procedure. You could say: "Alice and Hal, it looks like both of you are pressing for a certain conclusion. It seems a bit too early for conclusions. I wish we could review the issue again."

As a result of these interventions, members will see that a passing threat to the group's unity has been sidestepped and the team has repaired itself. Those who took the risks of dissenting and sparring will feel that at least they have been heard. Most important, the skillful management of conflict has the advantage of saving time and energy often wasted in valiant efforts to resolve underlying personality clashes between members.

> **MEMO**
>
> SUBJECT: Team building and productivity can be approached from unlikely directions. These include exercises and games for adults, the principles of play, and the managing of conflict.
>
> 1. Games should be introduced cautiously because they can backfire and appear irrelevant and time-wasting. But when prudently used, these games provide opportunities in exposing new facets of thinking, giving members a better understanding of themselves and stimulating individual and group participation.
>
> 2. Play offers the stimulation of surprise, risk and stepping out of ordinary life—all bordering on the activity of meetings.
>
> 3. Conflict doesn't have to drag down a meeting. Sometimes arguments raise members' energy levels. When this is channelled to finding areas of agreement or to finding more facts which support an argument, the meeting profits.

18:
Your Associates and How to Work with Them

Look around you and you will notice unique patterns in the ways members participate. For example, there are those who are good at connecting the reactions of associates. Others may be silent until a critical moment when they make an apt "clean-up" comment—bringing the solution closer to actuality. Some make cool, dry statements which may get lost. And there are some who speak so well, that they tend to "steal the show." These and many others are the associates you work with. Therefore, it's important to understand the working styles you encounter at meetings.

Find a Mate

While it's true that the most effective members find ways to work well with many different types, there's no denying the special advantage of teaming up with truly compatible members. Seek out those who seem to understand you immediately—who grasp exactly what you're saying and who share the same approach to the discussion. (However, don't overlook the possibilities of the opposite approach—developing an affinity for someone who has contrasting attitudes and working styles but who somehow complements you.)

These mutual and congenial arrangements ease the pressures and strains of a meeting. Think of the possibilities. You'd feel comfortable about saying: "I can tolerate your idiosyncrasies and you can appreciate my work style. The two of us have forged a compatible working unit—yet it doesn't exclude others."

Different working styles have been defined in R. Loevinger's *Annual Handbook for Group Facilitators*, ranging from the least mature to the most mature. If you think you're operating at one of the immature stages in the following descriptions, don't allow yourself to become disappointed or dissatisfied; you can raise your achievement level surprisingly quickly.

Maturity Levels

1. Impulsive Stage. Work is done for reward and no other reason. Other people's needs are not considered. Operates at an emotional, self-centered level. Recognizes his or her mistakes, laziness, inefficiency as bad only if this behavior is punished. ("I'll do things at the meeting only if I get rewarded.")

2. Self-Protective Stage. Accepts only limited responsibility and must be given continuous direction. Rules and interpersonal relations are manipulated for personal advantage. No capacity for cooperation. ("I'll do only what I'm told to do.")

3. Conformist Stage. Rules are obeyed to avoid shame or censure but are not fully understood. Trusts only those who are close, but not the "outsiders." Has limited ability to see beyond the superficial and material. Is motivated most by recognition for his or her work and possibilities for advancement. ("I'll do only what is best for my career advancement.")

4. Conscientious Stage. Rules are obeyed because of an inner morality. Has a sense of obligations and ideals. Not entirely in touch with his or her own inner feelings and those of other people. Can take initiative but tends to use self-criticism frequently. ("I'll do what is best for the company.")

5. Autonomous Stage. Is aware of own inner conflicts and conflicting duties. Can be tolerant of others' faults. Increased recognition of how to learn from mistakes. Is preoccupied with individuality and self-fulfillment. ("In what I do there are many contradictions between myself, others and the world. But I can tolerate this uncertainty.")

6. Integrated Stage. Follows model in A. Maslow's *Toward a Psychology of Being* of the self-actualizing person with superior perception of reality, and an increased acceptance of oneself, others and of the way life is. Can contribute to the meetings through spontaneity, richness of emotional reaction, capacity to be problem-centered (to give oneself to an idea without the self-centered "Me!" principle operating) and an increased capacity to give to other people. ("I am aware of my own uniqueness and self-sufficiency, yet feel very much a part of the meeting.")

Maturity Levels at Meetings

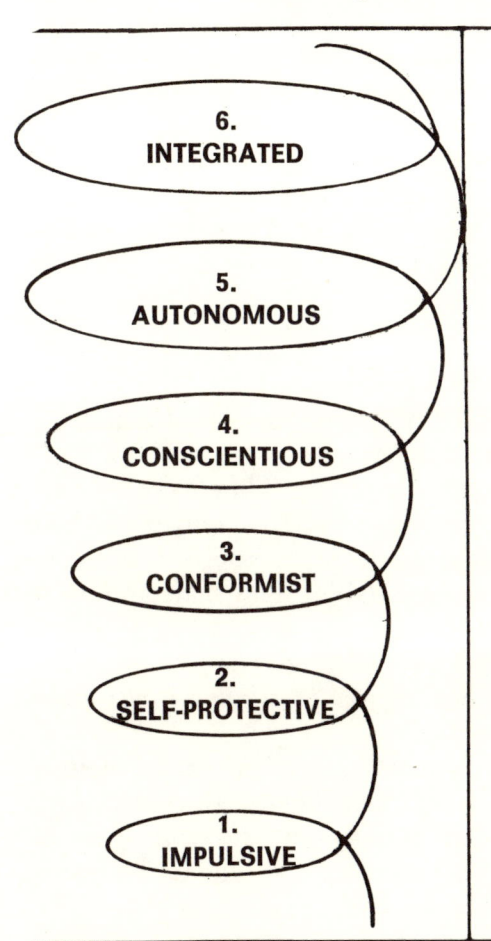

6. INTEGRATED	6. Superior perception of reality and firm acceptance of self, others and the way life is.
5. AUTONOMOUS	5. Strong desire to understand others to develop self and to tolerate uncertainties.
4. CONSCIENTIOUS	4. Aims to fill "obligations" to others and company.
3. CONFORMIST	3. Moves out of the shell but does only what is required.
2. SELF-PROTECTIVE	2. More involved—but with a few close ones who will help with advancement.
1. IMPULSIVE	1. Completely self-centered. Works only for reward.

The above classification is useful because it shows how your general maturity and behavior is reflected at meetings. As with most scales, there is much overlapping.

If you seem to fit within the first two levels (**impulsive** and **self-protective**), you have considerable work to do in building new assets to include: security, self-esteem, independence, reasoning, judgment and the perception of people and things as they really are. Self-preoccupation should be replaced with more contact with things outside yourself.

If you see yourself at the next two levels (**conformist** and **conscientious**) you've already developed a number of abilities and skills which enable you to do a good job of *centering*. You have enough feeling for others, insight into yourself, good judgment and capacity to endure passing frustrations to achieve a high level of productivity.

The last level (**integrated stage**) is the ideal to which you can aspire, but it's achieved by only a few. They have the ability to plunge into the experience of the meeting, to act selflessly and to choose the words and behavior which best bring out the potentialities of person, team and task.

Working Types

R. Heath's study of personality types, in *The Reasonable Adventurer*, is useful here. First he described the "noncommitters" —they're cautious, optimistic trouble-avoiders. They have an easy sense of belonging despite their tendency not to contribute their full share. On the surface they appear to be untroubled, self-contained and available, but not *too* available. The noncommitters would give this kind of self-description:

- *I've just begun a new assignment in the production department, but cannot say how it will work out. Any impressions I have of the new job are most probably premature.*
- *One thing I can mention is the helpfulness and friendliness of the others on the same floor, from the first day on. In return, they didn't seem to expect much from me. So far, everything seems harmonious and I intend to keep it that way. Not too much venturing forth for me.*
- *Several people going to lunch invited me along. I guess they realized I'm pretty much of a joiner because I told them how pleased I was to be a part of this organization. It was like being with the old gang. I could have, but didn't feel like collecting money, being the treasurer for the lunch check.*

Another type with which to compare yourself is called the "hustler." The "hustler" overlaps with the type called the "extrovert." The bustle, energy and drive for achievement are always there. But the hustler's weakness is in not being in touch with and accepting his or her deeper self. An expert talker, the hustler can explain things smoothly and logically. Friendships are sought out—but only to satisfy the excessive need for esteem from others. In the end, the hustler's aggressiveness and ambition don't yield the approval hoped for in the battle of life. This would be his or her self-report:

- *I am in charge of fund-raisers for a well-known, private, urban college. Never a dull moment. There is always the excitement of a new lead, and then the development of an approach to this source of funds.*

- *My friends and family always can count on me to join them actively, whether in play or figuring out a problem. But things have to be definite, not wishy-washy. I get jumpy sitting around and talking vaguely about feelings.*

- *My career is just right for me. I serve a worthy cause and do it well. Being with people is stimulating and enjoyable as long as they don't get too personal. I think there is too much of an emphasis on that sort of thing where there is no point or purpose to it.*

If you meet the next type, the "plunger," on a day when he or she's in a good mood, you'll enjoy his original, creative and colorful manner. Communication, however, may be one-way only, since the plunger's way is self-expression and free association of his or her own ideas. At other times, a gloomy mood will dictate an even more self-involved stance, perhaps of a theatrical nature. The plunger finds it difficult to be consistent and worries openly about difficulties caused by reacting in so scattered a way. The plunger lets you know where he or she is but it is not always easy to understand *why* he's there! This is the plunger's personal account:

- *In the "creative office" of an advertising agency I can work in spurts and bring out ideas at my own pace. This irregular production doesn't bother me—although it leaves the vice-president in suspense most of the time.*

- *Usually I have several things going on at once with friends and at the office. I guess I give the impression of never quite completing an assignment or defining and resolving a relationship.*

■ *Comparing myself to others, I notice that they seem to have their feet on the ground more firmly. At my age of 41, I'm still putting together my different "selves."*

The "reasonable adventurer " seems to combine many of the best features of the other types and may be recognized by his or her air to communicate sensitively and appropriately. Both playful and serious as he or she toys with ideas, the reasonable adventurer remains in touch with his audience. You feel comfortable with the reasonable adventurer's strong independence and compassionate nature. You feel his self-acceptance and some of this rubs off on you. He or she brings to the meeting a balanced ability to give and take, to let things happen and to make things happen. The adventurer's working behavior is like that of the self-actualizing person. This member, in Maslow's terms (*Toward a Psychology of Being*), has achieved balance, wisdom and rich personal and social success. This is man and woman at their working best.

These "working types" will, by no means, cover all the people you'll find at meetings. Rather they are meant to guide you in recognizing four approaches to life and work, differing widely from each other. The fourth, the "reasonable adventurer," represents the same ideal as the Integrated Stage of maturity described earlier in this chapter.

You may use this guide in two ways. First, by recognizing these members in advance, you'll find them familiar and easier to work with.

Second, try locating where you stand (or sit) among them. If, for example, you tend to be like the inconsistent "plunger," aim for a little more discipline and sense of responsibility—in a way that will not dampen your creativity. Or, if you resemble the "noncommitter," is your "untroubled" and "self-contained" manner really a mask covering your anxiety? This might better be handled by "biting the bullet" and taking some risks rather than looking "cool" outside but fearing the consequences deep inside.

MEMO

SUBJECT: You live in a world of business or organizational encounters. You must be prepared to deal with the various types of people you meet and work with daily.

1. In any one group, there are bound to be some who are well matched to your style of work. You can form effective working units provided you don't exclude others who wish to join.

2. Level of work and meeting style may be identified according to six stages: impulsive, self-protective, conformist, conscientious, autonomous and integrated.

3. Familiarity with various kinds of working styles—even if they're not compatible with your own—enables you to deal with other team members in an understanding way. Eventually this should lead to becoming more productively involved. Your associates may include: The non-committer, the hustler, the plunger, the reasonable adventurer.

19:
Midpoint Checkup

A midpoint checkup—glancing back and looking forward—is a unique and practical way of taking stock. What was done right? What needs correction? Where do you go from here? Such a survey yields astute observations by members about what needs changing, reinforcing or just continuing. It also gives the leader a prime opportunity to leave the steering wheel momentarily and join the others in the review.

The checkup is initiated at an approximate midpoint in the meeting. The leader asks members to take 15 minutes for shifting gears and observing what has gone on so far. Ask, "What do you think and feel about the meeting up to now?" Make it easier to begin—if there is a long silence with blank faces—by suggesting that everyone jot down one positive and one negative comment. After that, the review should flow easily.

The thrust of midpoint inventory is not to list a detailed catalog or history of the meeting. Rather, what you want is to highlight a few events of the meeting which merit comment. You'll find that certain areas seem to be brought up more frequently. They are: the Leader, the Content, Team-Building and Maintenance.

The Leader

Some members are particularly affected by the leader's style, especially where it does not match their own. One member was convinced that the leader's consistent tendency to be conciliatory dampened his own healthy dissent. Every time he had a challenging and useful encounter with another participant, the leader jumped in to "put out the fire" before it spread. This evaluation offered by the member proved to be of permanent value to the leader. She was flexible and secure enough to recognize that the flame she was trying to extinguish could be directed to "fire up" productive thinking among members.

A few more members' reactions to leaders follow:

♦ A member was disappointed when the leader did not help in clearing up a point, although many of the members struggled and floundered with it for some time.

♦ A member complained that the leader permitted too much wavering in the discussion, preventing a clear focus on the goal.

♦ A member didn't mind the leader's obvious preference for a certain pre-planned solution, but complained about the leader's refusal to vary his original intent even slightly.

♦ A member was bothered by the paradox of a leader who spoke reverently about the importance of member participation but who held the stage more than 50 percent of the time.

♦ A member was keenly aware of a mood of strain and discomfort which the leader never attempted to dispel.

Content—What Is Said

Better understanding of what is said at a meeting can be made when members are free to go back to unfinished or uncomprehended statements made earlier by themselves or others. These are examples of such attempts to retrieve or repair such disconnected messages:

"Jack said something earlier which I agree with only partly because I don't follow the logic of the last part of it."

"I have a question about something that was *not* included in Grace's report."

"Haggles spoke about so many things happening on his route that it was difficult to follow."

"I've been getting an impression that so far the task is too narrow. It has to be broadened to make it worthwhile to work on."

Team-Building and Maintenance

The quality of a meeting has a great deal to do with process—the "fittings," connections and relationships between events as well as people. Guidelines, such as the following, were suggested in the *Annual Handbook for Group Facilitators* (1972):

* **Participation**—Is it limited to too few? Is there too much jostling to get your voice heard?
* **Influence**—Is there undue emphasis upon autocratic leadership; deferential bowing to avoid trouble; staying out of the discussion entirely? Have there been adequate efforts to include everyone? Were attempts made to promote acceptance of others?
* **Decision-Making Procedures**—Sometimes, decisions are made without considering the effects on other members. Often, this happens when you make a decision and carry it out without consulting others. Or two members can "join hands" and push through their ideas. Or a majority may push its decision without bothering to achieve a consensus of all members first.
* **Task/Function**—Task/functions have to do with keeping the job moving and getting it finished. To do this, raise questions about the best way to tackle a problem and solve it together. Another technique is to summarize what has happened so far. Generating facts, opinions and feedback is vital for promoting clarifications and solutions.
* **Maintenance Functions**—These functions serve to keep relationships harmonious among the members. They can create a group atmosphere that allows each member to contribute maximally.
* **Group Atmosphere**—The general mood or spirit you should aim for is mutual respect, cooperation and concentration on the task. However, the atmosphere should be free enough to permit conflict and disagreement to rise to the surface. A meeting atmosphere that is all calm and sweet is not necessarily the most productive.
* **Membership**—The degree of acceptance or inclusion in the group can be crucial to members' well-being. Some members wish to work closely with others, maintaining close subgroup protective alliances. There are others who feel on the outside and

want to come in out of the cold. Still others tend to push themselves far away from the "heat," preferring calm to competition.
* **Feelings**—Are feelings recognized, accepted and expressed as part of natural give-and-take? Or are members spouting thoughts which are disconnected from how they feel?
* **Norms**—Is the spirit of a centered meeting carried out explicitly? Or is the meeting dominated by spoken or unspoken moods which impede progress? These may include such things as adhering to a pecking order, rigid politeness (which curtails honest disagreement) and avoiding any risk-taking.

What to Do at the Midpoint Checkup

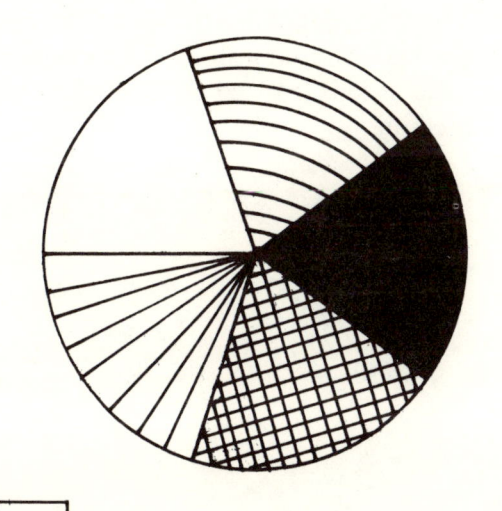

☐ Give leader feedback

▨ Give individual members feedback

■ Give and receive messages about developing and solving the task-theme

▩ Give and receive messages about team-building

▧ Give and receive messages about maintenance of meeting

If a midpoint checkup seems like a wasteful luxury, consider these vital advantages:

•• A chance for members to expand other sides of themselves—while the leader's authority is relaxed.

•• A refreshing change of pace from participating. Allows observing and evaluating skills to dominate. When a member takes a hand in the design of the meeting, it deepens the involvement.

•• Gives everyone an appraiser's "license" to do what cannot be done in the routine course of a meeting (where attention must be concentrated on the working out of the task).

•• Hindsight is converted into foresight. Lessons from the first half can be applied to the second half.

As the meeting goes on beyond the checkup phase, leader and members will become more attuned to where and how improvements are needed. The essential balance of the Member, Team, Work and Organization can be maintained. In this spirit, members and leader can carry the lessons learned from the first half down to the finish line of the meeting.

MIDPOINT CHECKUP

> ## MEMO
>
> SUBJECT: An evaluation at about the middle of most meetings has unique advantages. You can both glance back and look forward. Such a survey enables a thoughtful leader to take a rapid reading of accomplishments up to that point, and balance them against unmet goals.
>
> 1. The checkup provides a chance for you to examine your actions and those of others.
>
> 2. This review also sanctions questions or challenges directed to the leader about things said or done at the meeting.
>
> 3. The appraisal represents both a welcome change of pace as well as a fresh opportunity to become more seriously involved in the purposes of the meeting.

20:
First Aid for Meetings in Trouble

Throughout every meeting, aches, strains and floundering are to be expected. Sometimes these problems are self-corrective. But if the conditions persist, prompt "first aid" is necessary.

The following is a "bag of troubles" (warning signals that productivity is bogging down) and a "kit of remedies." The three areas requiring first aid are the Weak "I" (Member), the Limping Team and the Fading Task.

Weak "I"   When you're anxious about the give-and-take or the competition in a group, you're under stress. You feel weak and unable to function. You have doubts about getting enough protection and reassurance from others. You can't seem to assert your rights. On the other hand, you may show your uneasiness by talking too much or pushing too hard.

Limping Team   The team's energy is wasted when it goes off the track and singles out individuals for attack. At times, there may also be a loss of "team memory" about the need for consensus, rapport and commitment.

Fading Task   When the procedures and the structure of a meeting are neglected, the task is pushed aside and the meeting becomes disjointed and unproductive. The cohesive pull of the common task is lost. The field is now open for irrelevant personal agenda and other distractions.

The Weak "I"

The dysfunctional *I* suffers various "ailments," requiring different kinds of first aid.

Symptom: "Stiff joints"

Bending and changing are sure signs that members are adapting successfully. When you're threatened by change you're unproductive as you use valuable energy to keep tightly coiled and protected. Your "joints" become stiff. You require repeated explanations. Your objections to recommendations have a hollow ring since they are based on resistance and apathy.

First Aid

Call attention to these self-corrective axioms:
* I must accommodate to others.
* I can be receptive to new ways of looking at things.
* I can expand by taking more initiative for the organization rather than just guarding my own frontiers.
* If I become too comfortable, I may stagnate. I will try to explore new ways of dealing with people and situations on a regular basis.

If members are receptive to examining themselves in depth, the leader can ask for volunteers to recount experiences of their bending or changing at the meeting or elsewhere. The person whose joints need loosening may then make comparisons and use them to effect a change.

Another approach was used when Lee was holding up decisions about a series of relocations and space assignments in a new building. The leader recognized that Lee, a section chief, was feeling cast aside, without real cause. The assigned new location in the rear of the building had its advantages, but the section chief looked hurt. The leader said, "Lee! What is the worst that can happen if your section is located in the rear of the building instead of the front?" Lee thought for a moment and smiled. "The worst? More quiet to concentrate!" Lee was smiling in recognition that he possessed more flexibility than he was aware of initially.

Symptom: Uneasiness and silence

Dividing people into extroverts and introverts can be useful in understanding certain enthusiastic or long-faced reactions to meetings. Perhaps you work as well—or better—in company than when alone. Or are you more at home with yourself, finding rewards mainly in one-person problem-solving operations? If you're more introverted than extroverted, you may find that the meeting becomes almost intolerable because it demands your participation. Feelings of anger, detachment and fear tend to build up and immobilize you. Probably, your tendency is to withdraw for relief. Do you say, "Let others do it"? And do you tend to sink into silence? Rescue is called for.

First Aid

There is a danger of coming down too hard on yourself or some other "reluctant" team member. Generally, harsh judgments just increase the uneasiness and silence, and push you further into your shell. Instead, a reminder that everyone's individual interpretations of the task are worth being heard and considered eases tensions. And, at one meeting, several warm and generous members spontaneously devised a new remedy: They gazed in a spirit of friendly concern at Harold, who was not participating. At first, Harold blushed. After a few more seconds passed, he smiled. Then he addressed a comment to the concerned members. By the end of the meeting, Harold was exchanging freely with everyone.

Symptom: "High Blood Pressure"

Assertiveness, initiative and energy are important assets. But when they're overly intense, you develop a special kind of "high blood pressure." You become a monopolizing and boasting nuisance. You "clot" the bloodstream of the meeting. Sometimes, you'll even be encouraged to continue this behavior—when the team lacks the healthy resistance to balance your one-man or one-woman broadcast. At these times, though your own volume is deafening to others, you don't hear or realize how far you're pushing.

First Aid

If you or another member are using the meeting as a tool for personal gain, direct confrontation is the remedy. Expect members to confront you (and you should confront any members) whenever the meeting is being monopolized. Here's an example:

LEADER: Jack, would you conclude your point about our new product to give others a chance now?

JACK: (Taken aback, but continuing) I've been asked about my long experience in the field using this equipment—and I have a lot to say. Do you think I can continue?

LEADER: (Taking it a step further) Are there any of you who had something to say but couldn't get the floor?

JACK: (Without hesitation) I think I can wrap this up in less than 15 minutes, if—

LEADER: (Last-ditch confrontation, short of saying, "Shut up!") Jack, why do you insist on taking so much of our attention? I'd like to hear from the others now. I think you should keep quiet and listen.

Symptom: "Bitter taste"

A meeting is in progress where the task is to improve the sale of garden tools. Ms. Tucker shows her flow chart of steps in administering a consumers opinion poll. Mr. Garth, a skeptic of polls, objects to the procedure, yet admits, "There are advantages in analyzing sales records according to geography." The leader knows that Tucker and Garth are capable of resolving their differences. But suddenly Mr. Carr, who has a "bitter taste" after his proposal was rejected, snaps: "It seems to me that we are missing some people from the Finance section." Recognizing Carr's remark as not only irrelevant but as an attack on the meeting itself, the leader avoids getting trapped in a useless discussion about the presence or absence of representatives from Finance.

First Aid

The leader understood that Carr was bitter about a division head's rejection of one of his proposals. This bitterness was coming out in the form of an attack on the meeting as a whole. The leader decided to "play it straight" and bring in some positive facts. Reminding members that people from Finance had agreed that they didn't need to be here but that they'd be available to review related budgetary questions, if necessary, the crack was smoothed over and the meeting continued smoothly.

The Limping Team

Symptom: Abuse and strain

Sometimes one member is singled out for more than the usual dose of criticism. He or she is pushed into the target area like a rabbit at bay, surrounded by hounds. This can happen when members' disappointments and frustrations are ignored or poorly handled and team morale weakens. The wise leader is alert to this kind of "dumping" and restores a steady pull on *all* the oars.

First Aid

If you call public attention to this situation—without judgment or more dumping—most likely there'll be an immediate letup. Most "hounds" really don't want to be part of the hunt. That's why a sense of fairness is restored easily. Point out that the members are ganging up "10 against one." You may even say something favorable about the "victim," weakening the attack even more. Or the leader can gently chide the others with a comment to the victim: "Dave, can you tell us how it feels to be in the hot seat? I get the feeling that some of us aren't aware of what's happening."

Another instance of abuse and strain: The group was pressing Demetrius too hard at a recent meeting. The shipping manager was out of town and, as a result, Demetrius accepted too heavy a share of the load. Everyone shouted out their questions to him and the strain began to show. The leader applied first aid in this way:

"Demetrius, it's true that you're the *only one here* who has direct contact with the shipping schedules. But Sampson, as shipping manager, has several important missing pieces of information. He'll fill us in when he returns. Meanwhile, you shouldn't be expected to field *all* the questions—we should save a few for Sampson!"

In this way, a team forcing a member into an unnecessarily stressful position of carrying too heavy a load was redirected. First aid rescued the team—as well as the victim!

Symptom: Weak eyesight

A team must examine itself regularly and make its own "medical" checkups. But working teams tend to avoid this kind of self-care. One member may be afraid that he or she will be accused of doing something wrong. Another is concerned that his or her comments will hurt another's feelings. They move along with blinders over their eyes—only vaguely aware of what is going on around them. The result? A condition develops (weak eyesight) which keeps the picture perpetually blurred or dim.

First Aid

The leader should ask the members to consider the following questions:
* "What's happening now and what may have led to it?"
* "What can be done to improve the way we are going about our work?"

One successful way to get a good focus on process is to ask members to describe what is, or is not, working well for *them*. This first aid cries out for the team to examine and improve their procedures.

The following comments were made by middle managers of a large chemical manufacturing firm when asked to tell, in one sentence, how the meeting was working for each of them.

MR. STORCH: I work better if I know everyone at a meeting—or at least am introduced to them. There are three people here who are strangers to me. For starters, I'd like to know their names.

MS. ISTRIA: I was wondering why the section chiefs from Finance aren't present. They know some of the answers to the questions over which I'm wracking my brains.

MR. WEISGAL: There is something no one has explained to me. Why is management having us look into the Alpha Line (which is making a profit), if last month's report on the Beta Line was in the red?

MS. LONGFELLOW: Quite a few decisions already have been postponed. I'm wondering if we're delegated to make firm decisions and recommendations for the vice-president. I could join stronger forces with all of you if I got some signal that the people "upstairs" really want to use my ideas.

Stability for the demoralized team can be provided by offering members a chance for self-healing. This improves the "eyesight" and reduces blaming others for the faltering of the team.

Symptom: A Grumpy, Restless Team

Even before everyone sat down at a recent meeting, you could feel tension in the air. Members began having side conversations soon after the meeting began. A few people got up to change seats. Several speakers were greeted with irritated glances. There was a lot of movement but nothing was getting done. The leader tried to focus on the task-theme, which some members helped set up that morning, to no avail.

First Aid

The leader, sensing that there was more going on beneath the surface, saw that the solution had to go beyond calling these many distractions to the attention of the group.

The leader stepped down and *joined* the ranks by announcing his own dilemma as leader. With a troubled expression, he admitted: "I find it difficult and discouraging to try and figure out what's happening and what to do about it. There's something going wrong and I think everyone feels it. Can someone help put us back on the track?" Silence followed. But it proved how strong an impact this comment had on the group. Then one member suggested, "Let's start all over again from the beginning."

The leader transferred the burden of the problem to the team successfully by giving up the "know-it-all role" and showing his dilemma openly. When there is grumpiness, often team members are pulling in opposite directions. By showing that this problem could be handled by the whole team, the leader brought members together to work more harmoniously.

The Fading Task

First aid is also needed when the central importance of the task is lost.

Symptom: Loss of reality

When the task is rushed through the meeting without the necessary unfolding of facts, or when the leader seems to want to end the meeting prematurely, a loss of "reality" occurs. Members become reluctant to give or get information about the decisions being made.

First Aid

At a personnel department meeting, the leader was conducting the discussion at a careless, almost hectic, pace. Everyone seemed to be silently asking the same question: "Is this meeting necessary?" It was felt that the chief personnel officer merely wanted to rubber-stamp a decision that was already made by the Board of Directors.

Immediate relief in this case was given by an outspoken "old-timer" in the company. Katie Gray felt secure enough to bring the matter into the open in a diplomatic way.

"I don't mind reviewing the personnel policy of the Foods Division even if, in fact, we have no policy input at this meeting. But it bothers me that it's not out in the open. I don't mind being asked to screen and pick up major flaws in the proposal—so long as I understand the limits of what I'm supposed to be doing."

The leader smiled with some relief and said: "I knew that the decision on the proposal was already made—more or less—but I couldn't tell you this. It would have been useless to start a meeting in that way. I was hoping for an opportunity to tell you that I consider our job of reviewing the decision—picking up any big flaws—as worthwhile. I hope we can go on now with a clear signal."

The task remained somewhat diminished. But the members agreed to pitch in, having realistic expectations about why—and how much—they were needed for this meeting.

MEMO

SUBJECT: Early warning signs of trouble, corrected with specific measures, will prevent major strains from developing.

1. Trouble can occur when you or other members are under more stress than you can handle. This stress can be detected by underinvolved or overinvolved behavior.

2. The team may develop a "limp" when some of its members pull away—a result of disappointment. A team can also lose sight of its mission as a group committed to consensus.

3. Another weak spot is a neglected task. Once it loses its importance as a central focus, a flood of irrelevant matters rush in.

4. The leader is in charge of "first aid," providing welcome relief with prompt and soothing measures based on an accurate diagnosis.

21:
How to End a Meeting Successfully

When a successful meeting is drawing to a close, you feel pleasantly tired and sometimes even like you've won a small victory. No doubt, a victory over so many of the things that can go wrong!

Once again, as at the start, the leader must perform focal acts which no one else can do. At the close, the leader concentrates equally on the work done and on the people who did it.

The Work Done

- **The Information Leader.** Point out what material has been covered and shared. Go over the highlights. Remind members where the information has been unclear or spotty. Suggest why this has happened. State if, and when, a follow-up is needed to develop a better understanding of the information.
- **The Problem-Solving Leader.** Point out how the problem was first presented, how it developed and how and when it will be followed with active solutions. Go over the important differences that are still unresolved but which can be kept in mind for future meetings.
- **The Creative Meeting Leader.** Review the new perceptions and combinations of ideas that were hatched as a result of free-wheeling thinking and interacting. Give your opinion of the decision or product discussed—how it may or may not be applied.

♦ **The Teaching Leader.** List the knowledge, skills and attitudes that were introduced. Indicate how they fit the purposes of the organization and how members can use them in their specific assignments. Determine what still needs to be done to practice and review what has been learned.

The People Who Did It

To bring the meeting to a full conclusion, the leader should also focus on each member's responsibility to *assume control* over the task. Up until this point the approach was exploratory. Now the process involves not only making the decisions—but also carrying them out. To conclude the meeting, a bridge from exploration to commitment has to be built.

The leader can bring in a final review of the main points of agreement, disagreement and follow-up—as suggested above for each kind of leader. Members will see that actually they have been shaping and controlling the task all along—even those members who held minority opinions. Remind the "dissenters" that their views did, in fact, have a part in influencing the discussion and ultimate outcome.

In dealing with any *leftover feelings*, explain that there are bound to be some bruises following the risk-taking and self-expression of a *centered* meeting. Also, in a more positive vein, ask members to recall the many times during the meeting that mature emotions held the team together.

Many *leftover feelings* are easy to spot. For instance, if Jim looks deflated after debating a point too hotly, he deserves recognition for having followed his convictions. If Roger's eyes show he's holding something back behind his compressed lips, ask him to finish what he has to say now, rather than waiting until he gets home. And if two factions are still turning away from each other, ask them to place their agreements and disagreements in better perspective.

The follow-up is the leader's ultimate responsibility. Announce that the decisions will be conveyed to a specific person or officer in the organization. Or, if members are involved directly in carrying out recommendations, make the assignment when the members are present since they may have good suggestions about how the follow-up is done. Involving members in this way gives final proof that they have had a genuine stake in the meeting. If, however, you want to think over the assignment, announce it so that the follow-up doesn't become shrouded in mystery.

Record of Meeting

A brief written record of each meeting is the most efficient way of letting others in the organization know what has taken place.

These are the facts needed in a Record of Meeting. Prepare it as soon as possible after the meeting.

Record of Meeting

Date of Meeting:

Purpose of Meeting:

Results:

Action Taken:

Leader:

Team Members:

Department Head:

Adjourned

As leader, you addressed the members with an opening note: "This is my meeting, your meeting, our meeting . . . one part cannot succeed without the other." Now, at the conclusion of a productive meeting, you can say with candor: "We've been here together as catalysts, coordinators and conductors. If you and I have learned something, if a team has been put together, if a task has been done and the organization benefitted—our efforts have paid off."

MEMO

SUBJECT: How a meeting can end with a sense of completion, accomplishment and closure.

1. The work done should be summarized by the leader according to the procedures and goals of the format or shape of the meeting.

2. Since members are more connected with the definition and solution of a task than with its follow-up, they may feel a loss of control at a meeting's end. They may need the assurance that their input has indeed been of central importance.

3. If members have expressed themselves freely and strongly, inevitably there will be a residue of leftover feelings and thoughts. These should be acknowledged and resolved, if possible.

4. There are other ways of tying up loose ends. One is to ask members to consider what they've gotten out of the meeting, personally. Another is to assign follow-up duties based upon the work of the meeting.

5. A brief written record, agreed upon by members, is an efficient way of giving the meeting the importance it deserves.

Glossary

action
: The third stage of a procedure for dealing with disagreeable people at meetings. (See *awareness* and *decision*.)

awareness
: Three-stage procedure (see *decision* and *action*) for dealing effectively with disagreeable people at meetings. The first stage requires you to concentrate until you are fully *aware* of the quality that bothers you about the other person. In the second stage you *decide* whether this is a quality which you must reject or, in fact, wish to use. Appropriate *action* is taken in the third stage: Either discourage the behavior for its poor effect on the meeting or assimilate the quality for your own benefit.

balancing
: Flow of energy made possible by alternating shifts of concentration from one element of the meeting to another.

basic moves
: The five basic actions, or interventions, by meeting leaders:
1. Evoke—get members to respond.
2. Clarify—improve clarity and logic of discussion.
3. Support—give encouragement.
4. Manage—improve methods of working.
5. Self serving as model of self-expression.

body signals
: Nonverbal messages or "body language" which both senders and receivers can use to improve communication and working relationships among team members.

brainstorming
: An exercise to stimulate risk-taking and spontaneity in members. The team tosses out ideas at random, which are then listed, combined and utilized.

centering
: A method for achieving the clearest focus on the task of the meeting. Also, a method for making the most effective use of all the resources of a meeting.

circulation blocks
: Difficulties in sending an appropriately phrased message and difficulties in receiving the message intended. These obstacles are caused by lack of skill or temporary emotional interferences.

GLOSSARY

coaching — That part of the leader's function which encourages, stimulates, clarifies and resolves.

conflict management — The reprocessing of disagreements into an energetic search for areas of agreement or for more facts which will support agreement. Conflict is not avoided—nor is it necessarily resolved.

consensus — The preferred process for achieving agreement at a meeting because it is the result of a system of tolerating other points of view while also having yours heard. At its best, consensus allows everyone to emerge holding a piece of ownership in the meeting.

content — That part of a response which has to do with *what* is said, not how it affects the meeting and its members.

contract — Leader's statement of attitude, ground rules and general policy as to how the meeting will be run.

credibility — The degree of trust and belief you evoke in others at a meeting. You establish this through your profound grasp of the subject; belief in the meeting; honesty in expressing your opinions; and active participation with emphasis on the here and now.

decision — Second stage of a procedure for dealing with disagreeable people at meetings. (See *awareness* and *action*.)

design of meetings — The shape or form of meetings varies according to the predominant goal.

1. At a Presenting and Sharing Information Meeting—you inform members, with their active involvement, about important facts and developments related to their assignment.
2. At a Problem-Solving and Decision-Making Meeting—you find solutions and make changes related to procedures and products of the organization.
3. At a New Ideas Meeting—you create and develop new combinations of ideas and thoughts relative to the work and progress of the organization.
4. At a Teaching and Training Meeting—you instruct members in skills and procedures.

distractions   A member's attention is drawn away from the meeting by disturbances from within the person or from the surroundings. Such distractions are best dissolved—or sometimes used—when they are brought out and dealt with briefly.

encounter   Sharing and comparing the effect one person has upon the other. When not done belligerently, and when emphasis is placed on positive feedback, members can learn more about using their assets.

fading task   When the task is not properly maintained, or not centered adequately, its importance is reduced. A condition requiring "first aid" for the meeting.

family influence   Since a meeting sometimes evokes family feelings, a member should try to make use of positive influences, while suppressing the effects of negative ones.

foreground and background   This is the picture (foreground) and frame (background) to all we attend or perceive. Knowing the various ways in which the elements of a meeting may be perceived, members are in better control of their responses.

ground rules   Part of the contract of behavior for a meeting which promotes responses that are sincere, sensitive and fitting. These seven rules are firmly but not rigidly adhered to.

helping   In the independent and business-like atmosphere of a meeting, the act of assisting others may be neglected. Aside from the profit to the one being helped, the meeting as a whole benefits through these new working alliances.

human circus   The wide range of people we see at meetings who remind us in a jarring way of what we are, what we are not and whom we wish to be.

I-behavior   The emphasis at any given moment on any member's expression and representation of his or her needs and preferences at the meeting.

inner zone   The natural and spontaneous core of a person. Self-expression from this core is experienced by others as real and authentic. Excessive screening and defending against these feelings, particularly through the use of a façade or mask, results in detachment from others and loss of influence.

it-behavior The emphasis at a given moment on a contribution to the work of the meeting—to its content and/or process.

johari window An exercise designed to admit more "light" to see self and others more clearly, for better understanding and communication. This is done through mild confrontations.

leader The person designated to run the meeting, either by virtue of position in the organization or in recognition of special leadership ability.

leftover feelings The accumulation of tensions at the end of a meeting caused by the strain of managing and assigning thoughts, feelings and actions appropriately.

limping team When members pull away, or when the team loses sight of its mission or task, it begins to limp along. A condition requiring "first aid" for the meeting.

meeting A small group discussion with a common task, problem or dilemma, structured for maximum give-and-take among members. The leader helps mold the meeting design according to the nature and purpose of the meeting.

members One of the four main elements of a meeting. Hopefully, those who attend want to be there because they have something to offer through their knowledge, skill or ability to represent others.

midpoint checkup An evaluation at the middle of a meeting which permits looking back and forward. A unique and practical way of taking stock—and seeing what is still needed.

moderate responses Responses which are authentic and coming from the core (see *inner zone*)—but which are also selectively appropriate. They can reflect warmth, openness and sensitivity.

neutrality	To be unbiased as a leader, yet to be lively, imaginative—even somewhat transparent.
organization	One of the four main elements of a meeting. The body which sponsors the meeting, delegates responsibility and can issue rewards and punishment. To this extent, the organization has a strong effect upon the meeting.
phases of a meeting	Gradually emerging stages from pre-meeting to the ending. Leader should identify these stages to enable participants to fit their actions to the situation.
plan of meeting	Advance planning by leader and (if possible) members, to include: time and place; those attending; general problem; type of meeting; goals; specific emphasis; anticipated bugs and obstacles; the task expanded in the form of a *task-theme*.
play	A spirit (in a response) which may often be encouraged because of its value to meetings. It offers stimulation, surprise, risk and the novelty of stepping out of ordinary life.
present-oriented	The most desirable frame of time to adopt at meetings. In this state, you concentrate on what is really going on now and become free to function at maximum efficiency.
productive responses	Comments which build the task in any one of three directions: Cultivating—moves the member, team or task along at a steady, forward pace. Experimenting—moves the member, team or task in longer leaps by probing more deeply or by making comments which widen or heighten the discussion. Weeding—thinning out extraneous or irrelevant comments.
productive thinking	Your level of thinking can be raised by using free-wheeling (imaginative), analytical (seeing the separate parts) and rational (avoiding unrealistic assumptions) approaches to thinking.
reconciling opposites	An exercise to assist you in resolving two sides of an inner conflict. First the opposites are defined clearly and sorted out. This important step allows you then to make a less cluttered solution.

record of meeting	A brief, written report following the meeting, including purpose, results and action taken—to let others know what happened.
role playing	A dramatic device which asks one member to act the part of someone else. This technique has the power of actively revealing a lot of information to the "actor" about himself as well as providing an opportunity for understanding the other person.
self-actualizing	The ideally mature, competent, humanistic and self-fulfilled person, according to Maslow.
sensing and feeling	Using the senses and emotions to get in better touch with others. These functions are needed to bring out sensitivity, intuition and empathy—important skills needed to relate to others intelligently.
small group work	An exercise to stimulate participation by temporarily restructuring the meeting into smaller groups.
style of leader	Your characteristic mode of leading—from retiring to bold. Your style is usually fixed and relatively unchanging because it is based on fixed personality traits. It includes moving toward, moving against and moving away from members.
style of teamwork	An exercise designed to bring out not readily identified assets of individual members.
taking control	The strong inclination members have at the end of a meeting not to "give up" a task which they have painstakingly developed and brought to fruition.
task-theme	The definition, expansion and illumination of the task. This gives each member greater possibilities for connecting with the meeting in thought, feeling and action.
teaching-learning	Listening, presenting, reviewing, pursuing the truth aggressively—are productive activities which come originally from teaching and learning situations.
team	One of the four main elements of a meeting. In true team spirit members work together cooperatively. They put aside rivalries for the duration of the meeting—to accomplish something for the group and organization.

team building and maintenance	The kind of comment or action which has to do with *how* the functioning of the meeting and its members may be improved.
telling how it's done	Leaders tell members about the workings of a meeting with the aim of giving up to them a greater share of the event. The by-product is greater involvement and commitment of members.
weak I	A situation in which one or more individuals are under more stress than they can handle, causing them to become too little or too much involved. A condition requiring "first aid."
we-behavior	Emphasis placed at different times during the meeting on the functioning of the team.
willing and behaving	Behavior has to be willed with persistence and intention in order to carry out the work of the participant effectively.
work	One of the four main elements of the meeting. It comprises the definition, solution and follow-up on the problem or issue.
working types	The pattern and style of participation at meetings. Your associates may be seen as: the rival, the cooperator, the noncommitter, the hustler, the reasonable adventurer.

Index

Annual Handbook for Group Facilitators, 13, 21, 146, 154
Argyris, C., 24
Bales, R., 87
"Behavioral Impact of Leaders," 45–46
Behavior:
 experimenting with, 17, 21
 interpreting, 125
Berne, Eric, 25
Bion, Wilfred, 22
blaming and attacking, 87
body language, 93–96
brainstorming, 140
Communication:
 at meetings, 98
 blocks to, 99–104
conflict, 143
consensus, 30, 123
contract, 53–54
controlling and conniving, 87
Data:
 combining, 15, 21
 experiencing, 21
 sharing, 14, 21
demonstration interaction exercises, 139
disturbing stimuli, 165
Ellis, A., 107
Exit, Voice and Loyalty: Responses in Terms, Organizations and States, 30
Experience in Groups, 22
Feelings:
 left-over, 168
 reconciling opposites, 71
 shut-off of, 24
 types of, 108–110
Galwey, W. T., 73
Gestalt Therapy Verbatim, 91
Gibb, J., 27
Guide to Rational Living, A, 107

Heath, R., 148
Hirschman, A. O., 30
information, transmission of, 130
Inner Game of Tennis, 73
Interaction Process Analysis: A Method for the Study of Small Groups, 87
interactions, parent/child, 22–23
Johari Window, 140–141
Jones, J. E., 13, 21
knowledge and memories, 109–110
Leader:
 actions of, 46–47
 advanced planning of, 50
 as host, 52
 confrontation, 122
 definition of, 152–153
 lecturing, 136
 methods of teaching, 135–137
 neutrality, 63
 of creative meeting, 134, 166
 of information meeting, 130, 166
 of problem-solving meeting, 131–132, 166
 reinforcing, 136–137
 self-stating, 122
 styles of, 40–45
 teaching, 167
 teaching and training, 135–137
 team, 65
 types of, 34–39
Lieberman, Morton A., 45
Loevinger, R., 146
Lost on the Moon, 27
love and admiration, 87
Luft, John, 140
Maslow, A., 85, 147, 150
Meeting:
 action at, 113–114
 advance planning of, 50
 awareness at, 113–114

background of, 72
balanced, 79–83
basic actions of, 13
blocks to communication at, 99–104
body language at, 93–96
centered, 31–32, 55–57, 61, 66, 68, 79, 121, 130, 132–133, 142–143, 167
communication at, 98
creative, 132–133
decisions at, 113–114
definition of, 19–20, 106
demonstration interaction exercise at, 139
disturbed stimuli, 165
effective member of, 13
elements of, 20–21, 68–69, 73–74, 76, 79, 80–81
feelings at, 87
foreground, 73–74
generalizations at, 100
guidelines for, 154–155
information at, 130
insights into, 25–26
interactions at, 22
irrational beliefs about, 107
leader of, 20
maturity levels of, 146–148
member, 20
myths, 23–24
obstacles to, 21
participant observer at, 14
pecking order of, 63
personality types at, 13
plans, 51
play at, 142–143
preparations for, 12
problems at, 158–164
problem-solving, 130–132
productive blips at, 125–126
productivity, 23, 57–58
productivity exercises at, 140–142
realities of, 23–24

177

record of, 168
responses at, 89–90
rules of, 65–66, 89
summarization, 62
task, 59–60, 65, 73–74
teaching and training, 134
teams, 20
thinking at, 106–107
twosomes, 22
types of, 28, 31, 130–137
Member:
  applying generalizations, 16
  as participant-observer, 14
  as participant-sharing, 14
  beliefs of, 26
  centering, 31
  combining data, 15, 21
  components of, 68–69
  conflict at, 143
  consensus, 30, 123
  contracts, 53–54
  data-sharing, 14
  definition of, 20
  evaluating questions, 21
  experiencing data, 14, 21
  experimenting with behavior, 17
  generalization of, 21
  informal contact with, 50
  inner zone of, 85
  irrational beliefs of, 108
  knowledge and memories of, 109–110
  productive responses of, 120, 122–125
  relating to, 27
  sending and receiving skills, 14
  senses of, 109–110
  sharing data, 21
  shut-off of feelings, 24
  skills, 118
  willing and behaving, 110–111
nonverbal signals, 93–96
organization factor, 96
organization-solving, 21
participant/observer, 14
participating-sharing, 14
pecking order, 63
Perls, F. S., 91
personality, types of, 148–150
person-solving, 20
Pfeiffer, J. W., 13, 21
pleasing and placating, 87
Process Consultation: Its Role in Organization Development, 29
productive blips, 125
productive responses, 120, 122–125
productivity exercises, 140
Reasonable Adventure, The, 148
reconciling opposites, 91
Schein, E. H., 29
sending and receiving skills, 14
small group work, 141–142
Structure and Dynamics of Organizations and Meetings, The, 25
Task:
  background, 76
  components of, 69
  definition of, 65, 73–74
  elements of, 70–71
  fading, 164
  team, 80
  team-solving, 20
  types of, 122–125
T-Group Theory and Laboratory Methods, 25
Thinking:
  analytic, 106–107
  free-wheeling, 106
Toward a Psychology of Being, 85, 147, 150
twosomes, 22
withdrawing and avoiding, 87
work/goal factor, 69
work-solving, 20